Silent Paw and Pet Grief

A Practical Guide to Healing, Grief Recovery, and Coping with Pet Loss

Joyce T.

Contents

Introduction

Ever since my childhood, I've dearly loved animals. Growing up, I had a number of pets, but when I was around 10 or so, I was gifted the pet I've cherished the most in my life, even to this day. He was a beautiful Golden Retriever who I named Whiskers. I loved him with my whole heart, and it was clear he loved me, too. He followed me everywhere, napped on me immediately when I sat down after getting home from school, and spent every moment he could begging for strokes and attention—not that I minded, of course. It might sound cliche or a bit silly, but Whiskers was there for me when no one else was. Even if we couldn't talk, he made me feel cared for and understood.

Ordinarily, he was a healthy dog. He ate well, ran around, and loved playing with his sibling, the other dog we had. At that age, I wasn't super receptive to what dogs needed, but Whiskers was special. He was *my* dog, so one day when I came home from school, I knew for sure that something was wrong. Very wrong. Whiskers was uncharacteristically lethargic; he came to see me but not with his usual spunk, and he wouldn't eat, drink, or go to the bathroom. The vet didn't know what the problem was and gave him some medicine, but it didn't seem to help.

As a child, every loss feels like the first one precisely because many of them are the first. Whiskers was two years old when he passed due to medical complications, and he did so lying down next to me at the vet because his body couldn't handle the illness he had anymore. Needless to say, I was devastated. That was my dog, one of my first, and my best friend in the world. I would've done anything to keep him alive. Even now, he is still the most important pet I've had in my life because he made the biggest impact on me.

When we talk about pets dying, some people are less than receptive. To some people, a beloved companion you've cherished for years is "just" an animal and something you can replace. But I know that's not how it works, and you are probably coming to realize that, too. Even though pets are completely different from human beings, they make an indelible mark on our lives. They become members of the family, best friends, and our entire world. It's completely normal to feel shaken by their passing, to feel just as much grief as if a human you loved passed away. Not everyone understands this profound sense of loss, but I do—and I'm here to help.

In this guide, we will explore exactly what it means to mourn the loss of a pet, whether it was a furry friend, feathered companion, scaled pal, or another type of animal. Pet grief, the first concept we'll explore, is real, and the five stages of grief, which we'll look at next, are often also experienced when it comes to this kind of loss. From there, we will take a look at practical strategies to mourn and heal from this loss while respecting the life of the pet you're grieving.

Whether you've just lost a pet for the first time or have experienced this a few times—as is the unfortunate case with animals who have shorter lifespans—you deserve to grieve in a way that helps you heal. I see your pain, and I'm here to make sure you don't have to manage it alone.

Each pet matters, and so does their death. Feeling angry, sad, and even wronged are normal responses when they die, and it's important that you understand your reaction and what their passing means for you. The loss you've faced won't go away, but the feelings of grief don't have to take over your life. I'm here to guide you on this journey, no matter what it looks like for you, using the same techniques that helped me mourn the loss of Whiskers and the pets I've since had and lost.

After a lot of reflecting as a child—and even as an adult, despite how long it's been—I've come to think of Whiskers with love and fondness rather than sadness. When I think about him now, the loss isn't the first thing that comes to mind; it's his beautiful fur, his gentle attitude when we played, and his loving, kind heart. With the strategies I'll share throughout this book, you, too, can heal from the pain and find yourself in a better headspace while honoring the loss of your pet and remembering their impact.

With that said, it's time for us to begin our mission: helping you heal. Let's start by looking at a few key insights to help you make sense of how you feel right now.

Chapter One

Understanding Your Grief

Our pets are our family. –Ana Monnar

Immediately after losing a pet, you might not be sure what to think or feel. You might not understand why you are grieving or even *if* you really are, and the complex emotions surrounding grief can make everything harder to digest when it comes to starting the healing process. With this in mind, it is important for us to take a look at a few key facts about pet grief—mainly, why you experience it, the science behind it, and some misconceptions that can impact your ability to heal in healthy ways.

The Unique Bond Between Pet and Owner

Anyone who has ever cherished a pet will tell you the same thing: The bond between a pet and their owner is a unique, meaningful connection. It is not like having a partner, a child, or even a friend. Animals bring unique dynamics to our lives that are truly incomparable to the other relationships we have. Understanding this one-of-a-kind bond is one facet you have to understand before you can process your grief thoroughly.

Having said that, you may be wondering why pets and their owners have such a unique bond. What exactly drives that? It boils down to a few things. Most prominently, it is a matter of the nature of the relationship as a whole. Pets are often considered part of the family, even if they are a different form of family member. Just like siblings, cousins, and children hold distinct importance, pets do, too. They are often the ones who provide us with pure, unconditional love. They are friends and companions who, more often than not, are fiercely loyal to their owners. This special form of love and affection leads to a connection unlike any other.

Pets also shape our lives in many ways. For example, they become an important part of our routines. So many people post online about how they only hauled themselves out of bed that morning to feed a pet demanding their early breakfast. Although it can feel a bit annoying in the moment it's happening, that's ultimately a fulfilling and meaningful way to start the day. It is very special to provide nourishment for a creature you love, and that's something that becomes a daily habit. Walking them, playing with them, grooming them, and more are also instances where our daily activities intertwine with their life.

Pets also offer emotional support to their owners. Cats, dogs, and many other animals are incredibly receptive to the emotional challenges of their humans. Even if they do not understand why we are sad, they know precisely how to help, for example, by providing cuddles and affection or even just napping nearby. It is more than a placebo effect; many pets can actually soothe our minds and bodies directly due to their heartbeat and presence promoting a sense of calm (McGowan, 2017). Pets are also there when we need to rant and vent. They hold secrets better than anyone else on Earth and are happy to do so because of the attention they receive. They can also reduce stress and anxiety in other ways, making them an important part of mental health management for so many owners. This further strengthens the bond we have with our pets.

There are many people who have experienced these mental and emotional benefits. From emotional service animals to cherished companions who help people find a reason to keep going every day, many pets make a huge impact on the lives and health of their owners. Coupled with the fact that pets have their own unique personalities—no two animals of the same species act the same, after all—they feel just as much like family as anyone else does. This creates a bond that we cannot replicate with other humans, which is one of the many reasons why pets—and their passings—have such a huge impact on our lives.

Why Pet Grief Is Real and Valid

Pet grief is just as real and valid as any other form of grief. When you lose someone who you've held dear for any period of time, even if that someone is not a human, it is going to have an impact on you. The lack of affection and joy your pet previously provided can lower your mood directly, but there's something more at play. When you lose an animal companion, there's a sense of finality and permanence that follows, and because of the unique bond we just discussed, that's not something you can resolve by getting another pet or connecting with other people instead. This does not mean that healing is impossible; it just means that there is no bandage you can slap over your grief and expect to be healed.

When you lose a pet, many emotions can surface. Anxiety and emotional numbness can occur, for example. It is also common to feel sadness and depression. Sadness is a temporary low mood that can come and go in waves, while depression is more enduring and can feel like a gray cloud has settled over you and your mind. When either one is persistent, managing it is incredibly challenging because it involves a fundamental change in your brain's chemistry. This makes it difficult to "just get over it," despite what people who do not understand the struggle might try to compel you to do.

For many people, however, pet loss is accompanied by other emotions. Some may feel angry that their pet was taken from them, especially if the death was sudden, unexpected, or early on in their pet's life. It's not uncommon for people to not feel anything at all at first—something we'll talk about later on—while others outright deny that their companion has passed for a period of time. Whatever emotions you are feeling are completely valid, and your grief is real.

Debunking Myths About Pet Grief

Even if you know that your grief is valid, it's hard to focus on processing what you are going through when people are not understanding of your experience. Not all pet owners have the same deep bond with their animals that others do, and some people have never had a pet before. It does not mean that their lack of compassion is excusable, but it does explain why misconceptions exist. Identifying these myths and why they are inaccurate can help you combat them and push through moments of doubt when it comes to your own grief.

Misconception #1: It Is "Just" an Animal

A common misconception is that a pet is "just" an animal, so the loss is not that big of a deal. In a biological sense, your pet is an animal—that's a given. However, they are so much more than that, and there's no such thing as "just" losing a member of the family or a dear friend, even if that bond is not typical, like the connection between parents and children. If someone were to say that someone "just" lost a child or sibling, people would be appalled! You do not have to accept it if people dismiss your grief because your pet is not human. You deserve the same degree of empathy as anyone else suffering from a loss.

To combat this misconception, it helps to explain your feelings. Some people have not had the same experiences and are not sure how to empathize. They might mean well in saying that your pet was "just" an animal because they think that's comforting, but there are also people who simply do not understand. Explaining how you feel about the loss of your pet in a calm way, such as by using statements starting with "I feel..." can help get your point across and help others understand that grief is grief, regardless of who was lost.

Misconception #2: It Is Not as Bad as a Human Loss

There are some people who truly think that losing a pet is not as bad as losing a human they are close to. For them, the passing of a pet is not quite as serious as other forms of loss. The effect it has boils down to the personal connection we have with a pet, and not everyone connects to their pets the same. However, for many people, losing an animal companion is comparable to losing a human. I've had friends who have lost family and pets, and some have said the grief felt very similar but not quite the same, while others have said they grieved with the same intensity regardless.

Being told that the loss of a pet is not as bad as the loss of a human can feel dismissive. To manage this, let those around you know that even if it does not seem as bad to them, your pet's passing is still having a massive emotional impact on you. Let them know that even if they do not think it's the same, your feelings will not change because of a lack of understanding, and also explain that, instead, they can support you.

Misconception #3: Getting a New Pet Will Fix It

Another misconception many people stand behind is that getting over grief is as simple as getting a new pet. For some people, this is a step that can absolutely help with the loss; however, that does not mean that the grief they feel for a previous pet dissipates. As I mentioned earlier, animals have unique personalities. They can be shy, outgoing, sassy, and everything in between, and their personality cannot be found in a new pet.

In case someone raises this misconception with you, it is helpful to explain that if you were to stop talking to a friend because of a fight, you wouldn't be able to simply replace that person with someone else and expect the same connection. For some people, it's a huge deal to lose a friend, and they understand that they will not be able to replicate the relationship dynamic with anybody else, so this analogy is more effective than trying to empathize directly.

Social Attitudes and Misconceptions

Society often fails to understand or recognize the depth of pet grief, which contributes to the perpetuation of these losses as less serious. For example, when a human we love dies, there are conventions we turn to, like funerals, memorial ceremonies, and other common mourning practices, to acknowledge their passing. These norms are a big part of how we find closure after the death of our loved ones. When it comes to pets, however, similar rituals are missing, which can affect the way we see the significance of their death.

Another way that social attitudes affect how we perceive the significance of pet loss is through bereavement policies. For example, countless workplaces have extensive policies that allow for time off to grieve the loss of a friend or family member. Similar policies do not exist for pets, which makes it seem, in many cases, like overdoing it to ask for even a day off to grieve their passing. Because this time away from work—and effectively time to grieve as a whole—is not built into society nor deemed acceptable, it leads to the belief that pet loss is not a big deal.

The Emotional Roller Coaster: What to Expect

In the next chapter, we are going to dig into what grief looks like and each of the different stages in-depth; however, let's begin the process of understanding it with a preview of what the emotions you might face following the loss of a beloved pet can entail.

For starters, it is normal to feel an initial wave of shock and disbelief. When someone or something has been in our life for so long, it can be hard to digest that it is gone. A simple example of this is trying to check your phone when the battery is dead. It's a habit that's become automatic, so not being able to do it all of a sudden means your brain has not caught up to speed. Pet grief operates similarly, where if you are used to seeing your pet after work every day, your mind may take a while to process that that will not happen anymore—at least not with the same pet you lost.

It is also common to feel deep sadness and longing after losing a pet. You feel heartbroken because you lost someone you love, and in some cases, you could feel sad for the future that was cut short if your pet passed at a young age. Longing can stem from a desire to change what happened, from regretting not doing things differently, and from wishing that there was more time, even if only a moment. These are natural and valid ways to feel, but they can be intense.

Guilt and regret often surface for many people as well. It is easy to feel one or both for not taking an eager pet out to play that one time, for not noticing something sooner than you did, or for not changing something that led to their death. While it is normal to feel this way, guilt and regret do not necessarily mean you did anything wrong; in fact, it can be quite the opposite. I promise you, no one reading this book would intend to hurt an animal or take their life. You did not intentionally put your pet in harm's way, make them sick, or otherwise harm them, which is why it is important to work through this aspect of grief as you heal.

Emotional Fluctuation

During grief, emotions tend to fluctuate significantly. You might feel totally fine one day only to be hit with sudden and intense grief the next, and this can make it feel like you have gone one step forward and two steps back in your mourning process. This is not necessarily the case, as healing is not linear and can entail fluctuating emotions. Sometimes, this can look like sudden bursts of sadness and tears, but these emotional changes are not always bad. I've had moments where I experienced a change for the better very suddenly—like when I was a child and went from feeling heartbroken to remembering Whiskers's funniest moments, sweetest actions, and silliest incidents.

Grief also comes in waves because it can be triggered by reminders. Seeing a bag of food that you forgot to donate or toss out can hit like a freight train even months later, bringing back the ache you felt when you first realized that you no longer had a pet to feed each morning. It is not always possible to understand when this grief can hit, though. You might find a toy hidden under the couch and think nothing of it, only to see a photo of your pet and begin to cry. This is not to say that grief is unmanageable; rather, knowing that it can be unpredictable helps to handle it even better.

The Science Behind Pet Grief

For some people, it can be comforting to understand the science behind their grief. I know that, for me, it helped a lot to understand that there was a real, biological reason for my feelings; it helped confirm that I was not overreacting.

Physical Response

When a pet dies, the body reacts in ways that are strikingly similar to when a human loved one passes. The brain, body, and emotions are all affected, and the loss of a pet triggers significant responses in both the hormonal and psychological domains. Grief involves a disruption in the balance of several hormones and neurotransmitters, such as cortisol (the stress hormone), oxytocin (often called the "love hormone"), and serotonin (a mood regulator).

After a loss, cortisol levels in the body rise sharply, which can lead to physical symptoms like fatigue, disrupted sleep, and a weakened immune system. Studies show that the emotional bond between pets and their owners increases oxytocin levels, which is responsible for deepening the sense of connection (Marshall-Pescini et al., 2019). The loss of a pet can therefore lead to a sudden drop in the hormone, contributing to feelings of loneliness and emotional withdrawal.

Emotional Response

Something we've already touched on is that losing a pet can also lead to significant psychological effects, including depression, anxiety, and feelings of emptiness. Pets are often consistent companions and sources of emotional support, so their absence leaves a void in their owner's daily life. Many people experience intense feelings of isolation as well as challenges in coping with being in spaces they once shared with their beloved animals. The depth of this grief can be further enforced by society's tendency to downplay the impact of pet loss.

The Role of Attachment Theory

Something called attachment theory also has a hand in the science of pet grief. This usually relates to human relationships, but it can also be applied to the ones we have with pets. The theory describes how we connect with others. For example, it suggests that we tend to form strong bonds with those who provide comfort and security. Pets can offer this to us because of their unconditional love, which reduces loneliness and anxiety.

Losing a pet who served as an attachment figure can lead to feelings of abandonment, insecurity, and disorientation, especially in people who structured much of their emotional life around their pet. This type of grief often involves yearning for the lost companion and experiencing intense sadness because of their absence. In some cases, losing a pet can even trigger separation anxiety or panic attacks, particularly in people who struggle with attachment issues in human relationships as well.

Grief and Other Mental Health Disorders

Another aspect of grief to understand from a psychological and scientific perspective is how it can tie into other mental health problems, either by certain disorders developing as symptoms or due to unresolved grief.

One of the more direct ways that grief can lead to mental health issues is through something called prolonged grief disorder. This develops when someone experiences an intense, continuous form of grief for more than 12 months following the loss. This disorder also includes emotional pain, yearning, and an inability to return to normal activities. Because this form of grief is unresolved, it can lead to hopelessness, sadness, isolation, and more. It can even contribute to the development of other mental health disorders.

Another facet to think about is depression. While the two are distinct, prolonged grief can contribute to clinical depression. Although both can manifest as intense sadness, depression is characterized by a broader lack of pleasure in life, worthlessness, and hopelessness. If grief isn't resolved, it can result in feeling despondent about the future and disconnected from joy, which can lead to low mood and difficulties navigating daily life. In this case, depression can be more than just a stage of grief and instead become a disorder all on its own.

For some, anxiety disorders can be tied to unresolved grief or grief that isn't processed fully. Losing a pet, especially under traumatic circumstances, can make you fearful. And while this is normal, not managing those emotions can lead to overwhelming worry becoming consistent. This might look like worrying about the safety of others or yourself, experiencing social anxiety, or otherwise feeling on edge. Naturally, if ignored, this can lead to disturbances in daily life.

There are also instances where grief can manifest physically through pain, nausea, and similar sensations. While less common, psychosomatic symptoms, which are the body's way of expressing emotional pain physically, can arise. Unfortunately, this means that your physical symptoms can exacerbate your mental ones, creating a feedback loop that's difficult to break without dedication and, sometimes, professional help.

The Impact of Denial: Stunted Healing

So many people are delayed in their healing process because they don't want to accept that they're grieving. We'll get into this in the next chapter, but before we move on, I wanted to share a story with you to highlight why accepting and understanding your grief is so important.

One night, Lily lost Max, her beloved dog she'd had for eight years. Max had been her most loyal companion through countless sleepless nights and long, lonely weekends. But when he passed, her friends and family offered little comfort. They brushed her grief aside with phrases like, "It's just a dog," or "You'll get over it." Feeling as if her pain didn't deserve space, Lily tried to bury her emotions. She told herself, "It's only an animal," and forced herself back into her daily routine by pretending nothing had changed.

As time went on, she started noticing small shifts: She couldn't sleep, she was irritable, and she felt a persistent sadness hanging over her. Her friends would suggest outings, but she avoided them because she felt as though something inside her had become dim or weak—distant. The denial of her grief, hidden away and invalidated, had begun to take its toll.

One night, while cleaning, she found Max's collar tucked away in a drawer. She held it tightly and, for the first time, allowed herself to cry. Sitting on the floor, she whispered to herself, "I miss you, Max." At that moment, it hit her—she had been grieving, and it was okay to acknowledge it. She realized that by dismissing her own feelings, she had been stopping herself from moving forward.

Accepting her grief opened a door to real healing. She created small tributes for Max—a photo on her nightstand and a spot in her garden with flowers—where she could remember him meaningfully. Slowly, her heart began to lighten. Acknowledging her pain allowed Lily to truly honor Max's memory and find peace.

This initial understanding of your grief and what drives it is important. We are going to dive into the five stages of grief next, but this foundational knowledge makes it far easier to comprehend what you are going through and why, which can provide comfort, even if only slightly.

Chapter Two

The Five Stages of Grief

Grief is like the ocean; it comes on waves ebbing and flowing. Sometimes the water is calm, and sometimes it is overwhelming. All we can do is learn to swim. –Vicki Harrison

When you experience grief, there are typically five stages you pass through. They tend to go in order, starting from the initial shocked feelings you may have and then progressing to acceptance and recovery, but not everyone experiences them in the same sequence. Some people skip over one or more of them entirely, while others bounce back and forth between a few. Each stage involves unique challenges, and it is important to understand them so that you can understand what you may encounter as you heal.

Stage One: Denial

The first stage that many people experience when it comes to grief is denial. As the name would suggest, this involves rejecting the loss and being unable or unwilling to accept that it has occurred. When a pet dies, the pain can be so overwhelming that the brain instinctively delays processing it as a form of protection against emotional overload, and the mind may engage in various coping tactics to avoid confronting the reality of the loss. This is a natural and necessary defense mechanism that shields us from the immediate emotional impact of death.

For example, in this stage, it is common to feel as though the event has not happened, as if it is too surreal to be true. You might think, *This can't be happening*, or *I'll wake up from this*. This is your mind's way of creating space before dealing with the full emotional weight of the situation. It is also common to feel emotionally detached, as though you're unable to connect with the gravity of the situation. This numbness can present as a type of autopilot, where you go through the motions of your daily life but feel disconnected from your feelings.

Recognizing the Signs of Denial

In order to begin moving forward from this stage—as well as to understand why you feel the way you do—it's essential to know what denial during grief can look like. It's not always the same for everybody, but there are a few hallmark signs that you can look out for.

For one, when you're in denial, you may find it difficult to truly grasp that your pet is gone. You might imagine hearing the familiar sounds of their footsteps, or you may think they will still greet you when you return home. You could also find yourself downplaying the significance of the loss, such as by convincing yourself that your pet might simply be missing or will return, even though you know otherwise.

Another common characteristic of this stage is continuing your old way of doing things as if your pet were still alive. This might include keeping their bed in place, preparing their food, or maintaining their usual walking schedule. These routines help preserve a sense of normalcy and allow your mind to delay accepting the reality of your pet's death, but ultimately, they prevent you from processing the loss because they're a form of denial, not an intentional tribute or positive method of mourning.

Moving Beyond Denial: Strategies for Acceptance

Throughout this guide, I'll offer you various strategies for handling all five stages of grief, taking into consideration that your experience will be unique to you. However, I want to provide some strategies in this chapter as well to help you see from the outset that healing is possible and that there are concrete methods you can start practicing.

One way that you can work to confront your loss is by talking about your pet and the experience of losing them with close friends, family members, or even a therapist. This is a great way to break through the initial stage of denial. Discussing fond memories, your pet's habits, and the circumstances around their death helps to make the reality of the situation more tangible. You can also share stories of your pet to remember positive moments that make grief less difficult to bear at every turn.

Another option is creating a lasting tribute or memorial, which can help you acknowledge your pet's passing. This might involve planting a tree, creating a scrapbook, or holding a small ceremony to honor the pet. Acts like these are a concrete way of making the loss more real and provide a sense of closure that denial can delay. They allow you to say goodbye in a meaningful way and facilitate a transition into other stages of grief.

Stage Two: Anger

Many people experience anger as the second stage of grief. This is a significant and commonly misunderstood aspect of loss, especially when it is a pet who has passed. Though it can be intense and seem misdirected, anger can provide a way to cope with underlying emotions such as sadness, guilt, or helplessness. Understanding its role in grief can help you navigate this stage and make further strides toward acceptance.

Anger surfaces when we feel powerless or unable to control the outcome of a devastating event, such as the death of a pet. It's a method for the mind to distance itself from pain and allow for a release of emotions that might otherwise feel too raw or overwhelming. However, it often masks deeper feelings that are harder to express, such as immense sadness or guilt.

It is quite common for those grieving to be angry at themselves because they feel guilty about things they wish they could've done differently. I have experienced moments where I've been so mad at myself for not doing certain things that I was sure could have prevented a pet's death. In reality, it was not my fault, and even if I had done things differently, it likely would not have changed something like a chronic illness. These self-directed feelings often reflect a sense of responsibility for the pet's well-being and the anguish over not being able to prevent their passing.

It's also common to feel angry at others, such as family members, veterinarians, or the broader circumstances surrounding the pet's death. For example, you might direct your frustration toward the vet for not saving your pet or even blame a family member for not noticing signs of illness sooner. While this is misguided and unfair toward whoever it's directed at, it is common to experience anger and feel it intensely. It does not mean that you hate someone; rather, it is your brain trying to find an explanation for the emotions brought on by grief.

Sometimes, people feel anger toward life itself or even a higher power for the loss of their pet. This in and of itself can be guilt-provoking if resentment is directed at a deity the person believes they are meant to trust. To mitigate these feelings of guilt, it is important to understand that emotions like rage are a natural part of grief.

Recognizing Common Triggers for Anger

Anger isn't usually something that pops up out of nowhere when you're grieving; generally, it is provoked by specific situations or memories. Understanding these triggers and how they affect you can help you identify when you are most vulnerable to these emotions and learn how to redirect them more productively, which will improve your ability to heal and prevent damage to social connections.

The feeling of having no control over the loss is one of the biggest contributors to anger after losing a pet. You may feel powerless, especially if your companion's death was sudden, traumatic, or the result of a long illness where no treatment seemed to help. I've had so many friends tell me that a big portion of their anger was the result of feeling like they had absolutely no way to stop what happened to their pet or that they did not even get a chance to try. This sense of helplessness can spark feelings of frustration as you try to comprehend why your beloved pet had to pass away.

Memories can also contribute to anger during the mourning process. Memories of your pet, especially those pertaining to their death, can cause frustration to build up—particularly if your emotions surrounding the loss of your pet are unresolved. Even simple reminders like seeing their leash hanging by the front door or remembering a final day together can provoke you, but it's not always perfectly predictable. This is where healthy outlets come into play.

Healthy Outlets for Anger

While anger is a natural part of grief, it's important to find constructive ways to channel it so that you can prevent the destructive consequences of holding onto or misdirecting it. One option that's known to be effective is exercise. Running, boxing, or other kinds of intense physical activity can provide an immediate outlet for pent-up emotions because you get to burn off the adrenaline and tension that often accompany anger while also improving mental clarity and achieving emotional release. If you prefer something more soothing instead, yoga or walking in nature can provide a more calming approach that encourages mindfulness and bodily control.

Creativity is another good outlet. Expressing anger is an incredibly cathartic process, and activities like painting, drawing, and crafting can help you channel your emotions outward, which is both healing and meaningful when it comes to coming to terms with loss. You can also make these creations with the intention of them being a memorial or tribute to a pet, furthering their impact. Writing can also help by allowing you to put your thoughts and feelings on paper and gain deeper insights into what you are experiencing, patterns, and memories.

Managing Anger: Success Stories

This stage is often a tough part of grief to work through because of how strong the emotions involved can be. However, it's possible to manage the anger that arises when you're grieving effectively, and I want to share some success stories of my friends who have accomplished this as they healed.

First, let's talk about my friend Sarah. After she lost her dog, Sarah was distraught, and that quickly turned to anger for her. She was angry at the world for taking her beloved companion, angry at herself for not being able to control what happened, and even angry at her pet for leaving. She was able to transform her rage into something positive by starting a pet loss support group where grieving pet owners could share their experiences and find solace. This helped Sarah and others work through their anger and created a safe space for them to heal together.

Another one of my friends, Tanya, wanted to handle her anger in a different way. Determined not to let the emotion consume her, she looked up some coping strategies and discovered that gardening could be beneficial. From there, Tanya decided on a plan: She would create a memorial for her pet in her backyard. Instead of allowing her frustrations to fester, she put her energy into the project, planting flowers and trees in her cherished companion's memory and tending to the garden as a tribute to her pet's continued life. Over time, this spot became a peaceful refuge where she could process her emotions while also commemorating the life that was lost in a nurturing, positive way.

While anger is difficult and can have an immense impact on the healing process, there are so many ways that you can work through it and process what happened to your pet. It's not impossible, and I'm here to support you every step of the way.

Stage Three: Bargaining

After anger usually comes bargaining—a stage where you try to negotiate the what-ifs or plead with the universe, a higher power, or others to change what happened. Not everyone experiences bargaining, but if you do, it often looks like a preoccupation with thoughts of how the loss could have been avoided. For example, you might replay scenarios in your mind of the events leading up to your pet's death, imagining how changing one small detail could have prevented their passing. This is the mind's way of dealing with an uncontrollable situation by fixating on an element that could have been controlled, but it can increase feelings of guilt when you obsess over what you could have done differently.

Bargaining also often involves hypothetical deals you make with yourself or a higher power. For example, you might think, *If I do this, maybe I'll feel better*, or even, *I would give anything to have them alive again*. These thoughts signify the yearning to reverse the loss and bring your pet back, even though deep down, you know it is impossible.

The Emotional Impact of Bargaining

At first, bargaining can provide temporary relief to the extent that it offers you some sense of control over the situation, at least emotionally. However, the strain of negotiating the irreversible is rather severe and can take its toll over time. The constant revisiting of what-if situations can create mental exhaustion, where instead of spending your emotional energy on healing, you're allocating it to something that isn't helpful or moving you forward. Each time you cycle through this stage, you're confronted again with the reality of the situation—that you can't bring your pet back to life. Going through this over and over compounds the impact and affects your emotional well-being.

Bargaining also stems from a sense that you are responsible for your pet's death. Even if you feel like your actions played a direct role, it's important to know that it's not your fault. You would never intentionally bring harm to your pet. Thinking you're the reason for their passing can lead to bargaining because of a desire to change the outcome and be a "better" caregiver. While the initial sense of control this provides can feel helpful, you will eventually be reminded that not only is your pet gone but that you feel like you failed them (even though you did not). This weighs you down further.

Strategies for Coping With Bargaining

While bargaining is a natural part of grief, it's important to work through this stage to avoid becoming consumed by guilt and regret. There are a few ways that you can aim to do this.

One option I personally love is writing letters to the pets I've lost. When my grief was fresh, I would write about what I wished I'd done differently, my regrets, and all of the bargaining thoughts I had. This helped because it gave me an outlet to share with the pet I'd lost how much I loved them and what I would do for them. Over time, it also helped me stop ruminating on those thoughts and instead focus on healing.

It also helped me to reframe my thoughts. For me, a lot of my thinking centered around how if I'd noticed something earlier or taken my pet to the vet sooner, they might've lived longer. I felt responsible, and this weighed me down. However, I started reframing those thoughts. For example, I shifted the thought that I could've noticed sooner to: *I would never ignore my pet being sick, and I noticed as soon as I could. All I could do was my best.* This form of self-compassion helped me root my thoughts in the reality of the situation rather than in self-blame.

Stage Four: Depression

Next, you'll likely encounter depression, which is where things get tricky, as many people often bounce between this stage and bargaining or acceptance, which comes after depression. Working through it is a complicated process, but it's not impossible to navigate.

Understanding depression, a deep and often painful part of the grieving process, can help you recognize it for what it is and take steps to manage it. After losing a pet, the emotional toll can feel overwhelming, leading to intense sadness and despair. It is not uncommon for people to feel as though they have lost a part of themselves along with their pet. While difficult, this stage is a normal and necessary part of coming to terms with loss. It occurs when the weight of the reality of what has happened fully sets in and becomes difficult to bear.

Depression is not the same as sadness, although sadness is certainly a part of it. A lot of pet owners who are grieving experience an overwhelming level of sadness, but during this stage, it is usually coupled with despair. It is almost like a rain cloud hovering over you. Memories of a pet, which often emerge from a shaken routine, can make these emotions feel all the more prominent. Depression can also show up as a loss of interest in things that used to bring you joy. Even daily tasks like eating or getting out of bed can feel challenging, and the emotional fatigue that sets in can make engaging with the world feel impossible. Feelings of emptiness and social withdrawal are also common.

Coping Mechanisms for Depression

It is easy for depression to seem never-ending and relentless, but the best thing you can do is remind yourself that these feelings are not forever and that you can bring yourself to a place where they are not the most prominent point of your day. Similarly to the other stages, you can also work with a few different methods for healing from depression during grief.

When it comes to depression, breaking out of it can be an intense process because it is a chemical change in the brain, and it is incredibly resistant for many people. For this reason, I always recommend considering professional help if it is accessible to you. You can heal from grief without external help, but for some people, professional guidance is the fastest way to embark on recovery. Counselors or therapists can provide you with a safe space to explore your emotions, offer streamlined guidance based on your needs, and help you understand what you are experiencing.

Self-care is also a great defense against depression. For example, physical activity can help you because it breaks you out of the overwhelming feeling of not wanting to do anything, and the endorphins it stimulates can improve your mood and energy levels. Walking, yoga, and other forms of exercise are great for this. Hobbies and creative outlets also provide a way to re-engage with life. While it may be hard at first, doing something enjoyable or familiar can offer moments of relief from the weight of grief.

When to Seek Help

While for many people, depression due to grief can naturally subside through self-guided methods, there are also instances where it can become a more serious issue—one that is nearly impossible to manage alone and requires intervention. If you find yourself experiencing a more complex case of grief-related depression, it's important to know the signs indicating that expert help might be necessary. There's nothing wrong with pursuing this avenue, and it can, in fact, be lifesaving. So, what should you look for to know if you may need professional guidance?

One thing to keep an eye on is the level of sadness you feel. It's normal to feel sad, especially during the depression stage, but those feelings can—and should—subside over time. You might have days where you feel worse than others, but for the most part, your mood should improve over the weeks following the loss of your pet. If your sadness is just as strong or only getting stronger over the course of weeks or even months, that can be a big indicator that therapy or psychiatric guidance may be ideal for you.

Also, grief is known to disrupt daily functioning. This is normal for a while, and it's good to give yourself grace and self-compassion while you take some time for yourself. However, for the most part, people are able to return to day-to-day life and tasks related to hygiene, work, school, and more within a few days or a couple of weeks, depending on the type of loss and impact. If you notice that you're unable to get back to normal life after a while and that you're picking up on social, financial, or physical problems, then professional guidance might be in your best interest.

Another normal aspect of grief is feeling sorrowful or experiencing yearning and similar emotions in full. However, you might require professional help if you notice that they are turning into despair, hopelessness, or other severe emotions that impact your ability to experience the world in positive, healthy ways. It's important to reach out to someone for support, especially if these feelings persist, so that you can access the tools and resources needed to manage depression effectively.

There are many other indicators that might signify the need for professional help when it comes to depression. Some other areas to keep an eye on include:

- **Physical symptoms:** Depression can manifest through physical symptoms, which are often overlooked. Fatigue, lack of energy, disrupted sleep, changes in appetite, unexplained aches, or gastrointestinal issues may all point to depression, especially if they persist. If you spot them in your own life, it might be a sign that professional help can improve your healing process.

- **Isolation or withdrawal:** Depression can also come along with self-isolation or withdrawal from social connections. This is often a way to help with processing emotions because spending time alone can give you the space you need to reflect. However, if you spend too long withdrawn from friends, family, and others, it can worsen depression. Working to strengthen your social ties, attending support groups, or pursuing similar strategies can help.

- **Self-destructive or risky behaviors:** Coping with grief can sometimes lead people to engage in risky behaviors, such as substance use, excessive spending, reckless behaviors in general, and more. Such unhealthy coping mechanisms mask the pain without addressing root issues, which can be dangerous. If you feel compelled to engage in behaviors like these, it's essential to reach out for support.

Stage Five: Acceptance

The final stage is best described as the acceptance of a loss and the breaking free from grief that accompanies it. This is not the same as moving on or forgetting about your pet. Rather, it's coming to a state of peace with that loss that allows you to embrace the new normal you have without them. It involves a life that includes both the love and memories of the pet as well as the ongoing experience of coming to terms with their death. The goal of acceptance is to integrate the loss into life in a way that allows you to continue living fully, even as you honor your pet's memory.

Signs of Acceptance

It can be difficult to know what acceptance looks like, but there are a few key indicators that you might be approaching this stage. One of the most significant signs of acceptance is being able to look back on memories of the pet you've lost with fondness and even a smile rather than immediate sorrow. The intense pain of earlier stages begins to subside, and the focus shifts from the sadness of loss to the joy of having shared a life with your animal companion. This does not mean that you never get sad about losing them; it means that you now have a balance between heartache and warm, positive recollections of your pet.

Another big indicator of acceptance is when your daily life and other responsibilities start to feel manageable. You might notice yourself creating new habits and routines that reflect your current reality, which is a good thing. This does not mean that you've forgotten your pet, but rather that you have a renewed sense of purpose and structure that will allow you to rejoin life in a way that feels less negative.

Nurturing Acceptance

It takes time to get to this point, but you can proactively work toward creating a mindset of acceptance. One way to do this is by implementing routines that honor the memory of your pet. This might include lighting a candle in their honor or visiting a special place where they loved to play. These small acts of remembrance help keep their memory alive while creating new ways to adapt to life without them. You can make small routines like this a weekly or monthly ritual where you reflect on your pet and remember them fondly while also accepting their passing.

Although it can be hard to imagine enjoying life again after losing a pet, doing things that bring you fulfillment is necessary when it comes to reaching acceptance. You can work toward this by engaging in activities you used to enjoy, picking up a new hobby, spending time in nature, volunteering, or otherwise participating in whatever brings you a sense of balance and connection.

Moving Between Stages: It's Okay to Regress

Grief is not a straight line. While the stages we've just discussed—denial, anger, bargaining, depression, and acceptance—can provide a helpful understanding of what you might experience, they are not a rigid sequence. Grief is highly individual and nonlinear, meaning that it's perfectly normal to move back and forth between stages or to experience multiple stages simultaneously. Understanding that regression is a natural part of the process can help you approach your healing journey with more self-compassion and less frustration.

Common Reasons for Regression

There are a lot of reasons why you might bounce between stages. Even long after your pet has passed, unexpected reminders can reignite feelings of sadness or anger. A stray toy found under the couch, a picture discovered in a drawer, or the sight of another animal that resembles your lost pet can all trigger a resurgence of grief. These moments can take you by surprise and cause you to feel like you've regressed in your healing. This is normal to experience.

Anniversaries or special dates like birthdays can also bring up negative feelings and make some days harder to bear than others. While this is not unusual, you can also work toward using those dates to remind yourself of the positive experiences you had with your pet. A birthday can be turned into an occasion to volunteer and support other animals at a shelter, for example, which creates a legacy of caring for other animals in honor of your late pet.

Follo's Story

In honor of two of my very good friends and to help you understand how grief can be complex, I want to tell the story of their dog. Follo passed away before I started writing this book. They adopted him from a shelter, knowing that if they did not, he would have been put down because the center was out of space. To many people, Follo was not a first-choice puppy—he was small and not conventionally cute, but my friends saw something special in him, so they took him home.

Follo's life had gotten off to a rough start. He was aggressive due to a previous owner who hadn't treated him well, and my friends struggled to adjust him to their home at first. However, thanks to their unwavering love, patience, and care, Follo soon became one of the loveliest, most loyal, and most affectionate dogs you could ever know. He was perfect for them; he stood with them during the ups and downs of life, and he was a fierce protector of their daughter from the time she was born.

He lived a lovely, joyous, and long life of 15 years before passing. Follo's death was heartbreaking for my friends. He was not just a dog; he was their first child, their family, and their best friend. Even though they have good days, my friends still fiercely miss Follo and feel the grief that follows his loss, which is completely normal for pet owners to experience.

As someone grieving a pet, you don't have to feel like the end of your grief has a deadline or due date. You, just like my friends, are allowed to mourn for as long as you need to. With an understanding of what that process can look like, it can be easier to navigate your journey toward healing.

Chapter Three

Practical Strategies for Healing

*There is beauty in the journey, regardless of
the outcome. Let's grieve and hope, and fight
together.* –Marie White

With an understanding of the process of grief fresh
in your mind, you may be wondering what it
takes to begin healing. In other words, how can you get
the process started and maintain momentum? It requires
patience with yourself, dedication, and some practical
strategies that support your recovery from loss. Together,
we are going to delve into practical methods that have
helped many others experiencing the loss of a beloved pet
to help you begin to find a sense of healing and peace.

Creating a Daily Grief Ritual

Daily grief rituals are a good way to begin the healing process. They can offer you a sense of comfort, consistency, and purpose, and they play a significant role in healing beyond that. Grief can feel chaotic or unpredictable, which can make us feel lost. Rituals that are consistent can help us regain a sense of control and stability that reduces the anxiety and overall disruption caused. Having these routines also helps you integrate grief by normalizing the experience.

Furthermore, setting aside time to truly experience the emotions that surface and mourn rather than being blindsided by feelings of sadness, numbness, or anger at random means that you can experience your emotions fully without putting pressure on yourself to process them faster. Having a designated time also means that you do not have to worry about other responsibilities distracting you from your healing.

Different Types of Daily Grief Rituals

Grief does not have many bright sides, but one positive that it has is how versatile processing it can be. You are not limited when it comes to the ways you are able to grieve, which means your daily rituals can be anything that you want them to be. To help you determine what you may want to try, let's discuss a few types of daily rituals you can consider.

In addition to morning meditations being a peaceful way to begin your day, spending a few moments focusing on the memory of your pet can be a grounding practice that allows you to process your grief. One example of how you can carry this ritual out is by making it a daily habit to sit in a soothing place and meditate on your pet's memory. You can even use a guided meditation—there are many available online—to help direct you.

You can also opt to light a candle in your pet's memory. This is a symbolic act that can remind you of their enduring presence in your heart. This can fit into any part of your day or be performed as needed when you want to connect with the memory of them. Spending a few moments with the candle while thinking about your pet can help you process your feelings and normalize their absence. As painful as this can be, the reality of living without your pet can become comforting over time as you realize this is not a precursor to forgetting them but rather an act of honoring the presence they had in your life while they were living.

If your pet enjoyed being outside, spending time in some of their favorite places can provide you with a feeling of closeness to them and nature as well, which is great for finding solace and grounding. A daily walk is an example of an activity you can turn into a small ritual to honor their memory, as even without their physical presence, revisiting familiar routes can evoke a sense of connection.

Journaling can be helpful, too. It is a therapeutic outlet that a lot of people find value in when they are grieving. Writing a short daily letter to your pet, for instance, can help with healing. You can express anything here—memories, emotions, gratitude, or even day-to-day updates that your pet would have experienced. Over time, this practice can help you work through unresolved feelings and create a lasting tribute to the bond you shared.

Step-By-Step Instructions for Establishing a Ritual

Creating a ritual might not seem like the easiest process in the world, but you can follow these steps to get started with establishing one for your journey:

1. **Pick a time and place:** The key is to make when and where you perform your ritual sacred. Pick a time that works best for you, whether it's in the morning to start your day with reflection or in the evening to wind down. The place can be anywhere that feels peaceful and private.

2. **Pick meaningful activities or symbols:** The activity you choose should resonate with you and your relationship with your pet. This could be lighting a candle, meditating, writing in a journal, or taking a walk. You can also incorporate objects or symbols that remind you of them, like their collar, a photo, or a favorite toy. Choose elements that bring comfort and make the ritual feel personal and connected.

3. **Maintain the ritual:** It's important to commit to your ritual, even on days when it feels difficult. Establishing a routine takes time, but the consistency of engaging with your grief each day will help foster emotional healing. What feels right in the early stages of grief may evolve over time, so give yourself permission to adapt the ritual as needed. The important thing is to remain com-

passionate toward yourself and allow the ritual to develop with your emotional needs.

Using Journals and Prompts to Process Emotions

Another practical strategy that is empowering and useful for healing is journaling. Journaling gives you a safe place to write about the emotions you are experiencing as you process your loss. Putting your thoughts down can also be a tangible way to experience grief, and it leads to greater self-awareness, emotional release, and, ultimately, healing. When you journal on a regular basis, you are giving yourself the time and space to process each emotion you feel, you have a way to look back at your progress, and you do not have to worry about keeping all of those emotions locked up in your head or trapped in your body.

Journal Prompts for Pet Grief

You can journal about anything in the world, whether what you want to write about is your pet and memories you have of them or just how your day went. For me, one of the hardest parts of starting was simply figuring out what to say, which is why I love journal prompts. Here are some that are specifically focused on pet grief that you can work with if you are unsure of what to write about:

- Describe your favorite memory with your pet. What made that moment so special?

- What are three things you miss most about your pet, and why?

- If your pet could speak to you now, what do you think they would say? How would you respond?

- How has losing your pet changed your daily routine? What do you miss about having them in your day-to-day life?

- What lessons did your pet teach you about love, companionship, or life?

- Write a letter to your pet in which you express any unresolved feelings or things you wish you could say to them now.

- How do you think your pet would want you to remember them? What do you think they would want for you moving forward?

- Describe the moment you first met your pet. How did you feel, and what were your hopes for your time together?

- What are some ways you have noticed your pet's absence, both big and small? How have you coped with those instances?

- Reflect on how your pet comforted you during difficult times. How did their presence impact your emotional well-being?

- What do you think your pet's favorite thing about being with you was? How did you show them love in return?

- If you could relive one day with your pet, which day would you choose and why?

- What are some of the happiest moments you shared with your pet, and how do those memories make you feel now?

- How have you honored your pet's memory so far? Is there anything else you would like to do to pay tribute to them?

- What emotions have surprised you the most during your grieving process? How have you dealt with them?

- Describe how you felt in the days leading up to your pet's passing. If you knew it was coming, what was that time like for you emotionally?

- What do you miss most about your pet's personality? Was there a specific quirk or habit that brought you joy?

- How has the loss of your pet affected your relationships with other people or animals in your life?

- If you believe in an afterlife or spiritual connection, how do you envision your pet's spirit continuing? What brings you comfort when you think about their afterlife?

- Write about the first time you realized your pet was gone. What emotions did you experience, and how have they evolved over time?

Making Journaling a Regular Habit

Journaling practices work best when you turn them into a regular habit, as the benefits build upon each other over time. At the same time, it can be hard to adopt a new habit when you are in the midst of grief. I understand how this feels, so I want to share a few tips that helped me establish a regular practice for myself when I was grieving the loss of pets I've had.

First, it helped me a lot to pick a regular time. When journaling was already in my schedule, it felt less like something to squeeze in and more like a purposeful method for healing that had an important part in my life. I like to journal in the evenings, when my emotions tend to be strongest; you, however, might find more value in doing it at some other point in the day, and that's completely alright. Picking a time where you can spend 5–10 minutes writing helps establish the habit and is a way to carve out time specifically for healing.

Something else that helped was picking the right environment. Finding a place that felt comfortable and that was quiet was so helpful because I could feel at ease and not be distracted during my journaling time. For me, this was a cozy spot next to a window, but you might want to pick a different place or even head outside. In this space, I kept my journal and items I would use, like pens, which made it easier to just write instead of worrying about getting everything I'd need together first.

Finally, it was important for me to come to terms with imperfections in my journaling. I felt such strong pressure to make my entries perfect: I needed my handwriting to be absolutely legible, each entry had to be organized, and they all needed to be structured the same... or so I thought. Your journal is not supposed to be perfect—it is a place where you can jot down your most private, chaotic thoughts, and you should not feel judged, even by yourself, when you write. One way I broke out of this was by being messy on purpose—scribbling on pages randomly or writing overtop entries. This made it easier to break away from the perfectionism I was struggling with.

Exercise and Physical Activity for Emotional Relief

Physical activity and exercise can also be a massive support when it comes to managing the emotional challenges of grief. Exercise can be helpful in several different ways. For example, it releases endorphins—chemicals in the brain that act as natural mood elevators. These hormones help to reduce feelings of sadness and despair, making it easier to cope with grief. Also, exercise can reduce the production of cortisol, the hormone responsible for stress, thus helping to alleviate the overwhelming emotions that often accompany loss.

Beyond that, exercise can be a distraction from the stress and anxiety that you might be feeling. These emotions can show up in a few ways in your body, including muscle tension, fatigue, or insomnia. Exercise works against these symptoms by promoting relaxation and improving your health. Physical activity can also help distract you from your thoughts when you need a break from the feelings that accompany grief.

Types of Physical Activities for Emotional Relief

Different types of exercise can offer their distinct benefits, and it is important to find activities that are enjoyable to you and fit into your schedule in a manageable way. Some types of exercise you might want to consider include:

- **Yoga and stretching:** Yoga and stretching exercises are beneficial in a lot of ways. These activities are mindfulness-based, which means they encourage you to stay present and connect with your body through movement. Plus, the deep breathing and slow, deliberate movements can help relieve tension and enhance your state of calm.

- **Running or jogging:** Running and jogging are brisker forms of exercise that can be great for releasing built-up stress and energy. They both boost endorphins and are often done outside, which can be grounding, provide connection, and reduce feelings of anxiety.

- **Group fitness classes:** Group fitness classes are another wonderful option because they combine physical activity and the support of a community. Exercising with others offers a sense of belonging, which can be especially comforting when you are experiencing the loneliness of grief. Connecting socially through a shared physical activity can also reduce feelings of isolation and help you create new routines.

Of course, if there's a form of exercise you'd rather try or find more beneficial, go for it! Your grieving process does not have to look exactly like mine, and as long as you find coping mechanisms that are healthy and support your needs, you are on the right track.

Incorporating Exercise Into Daily Routines

Like journaling, it might feel tricky to incorporate exercise into your daily routine if it's new to you. I have some strategies for that, too. For example, it is important to set a goal for your fitness regimen. At the same time, what you're aiming for should also be achievable. It is tempting to set extraordinary goals that challenge you, but if they are unachievable, they will not make you feel any better. Pick a target, like exercising for 10 minutes a day, and steadily find ways to work toward it. If needed, you can always change it later on.

Something that helped one of my friends was finding a workout buddy to keep her on track. It is easier to work on a goal when it is a mutual effort, so having an accountability partner who you can exercise with makes it more difficult not to show up. You can ask someone who's also grieving or a friend who's willing to go on walks with you. This approach means that you do not feel alone while exercising and have the encouragement you need to keep making progress.

If you have the ability to, it also helps to try being active outside. The benefits of nature can make exercise feel more worthwhile and increase your determination to stick with the habit.

Soothing Yoga Flow for Grief

I mentioned that yoga can be helpful for grief. This is because it's a calming, grounding practice that can draw your attention to the present while improving your mood through physical activity. If you're looking for a way to get going, you can use this simple, soothing flow as a place to start:

1. Sit comfortably on your yoga mat with your legs crossed, your spine tall, and your shoulders relaxed. Place one hand on your chest and the other on your belly to start with mindful breathing. Inhale deeply through your nose, filling your belly, and then slowly exhale through your nose.

Focus on the rise and fall of your abdomen and chest. This deep breathing helps ground you by calming your nervous system and preparing your mind for movement.

2. From a kneeling position, bring your big toes together, open your knees wide, and lower your torso forward, allowing your forehead to rest on the mat. Stretch your arms in front of your head or rest them by your sides. Continue breathing deeply, and with each inhale, feel your back expand. As you exhale, sink deeper into the mat and let go of any tightness in your body.

3. Move to all fours with your hands under your shoulders and your knees under your hips. Inhale to arch your spine, lifting your chest and tailbone—this is cow pose. To shift into cat pose, exhale to round your spine into a curve, tucking your chin and tailbone as you do. Move slowly as you focus on the sensation in your spine, synchronizing each movement with your breath.

4. Next, stand with your feet hip-width apart and slowly hinge at the hips to allow your torso to

lengthen downward. Let your arms hang or gently clasp each elbow with the opposite hand. Bend your knees slightly if needed for comfort. As you inhale, lengthen your spine slightly. Exhale deeply to allow any emotions to flow downward and out.

5. From an all-fours starting point, walk your hands forward while keeping your hips over your knees, and then lower your chest toward the mat, bringing your forehead or chin to rest. With each exhale, allow your heart to soften toward the mat to invite release and vulnerability.

6. Lie flat on your back with arms by your sides, palms up, and legs extended. Close your eyes and imagine a calming, safe space—like a forest, beach, or garden. Envision yourself surrounded by peace and warmth. As you embrace the comfort of this mental space, feel your body soften with each inhale. Allow yourself to simply be in this moment, releasing any lingering grief and inviting a sense of lightness.

Mindfulness and Meditation Practices

Adopting a mindfulness and meditation practice can be a great help as you heal. Both can encourage you to direct your awareness to the present moment. Because you are steering your thoughts away from rumination over the past or fear of the future, focusing on the present can combat the anxiety, worry, and lack of control you might feel as you grieve.

Furthermore, meditation can help you become more aware of your emotional states, including the feelings that accompany grief. This might be troubling to hear, especially if you're afraid of acknowledging your emotions; however, mindfulness means not just confronting those emotions but accepting them as well. Instead of pushing the feelings away, meditation teaches you to sit with them, creating a compassionate space for processing your grief.

Step-By-Step Instructions for Basic Mindfulness Exercises

Mindfulness and meditation practices don't need to be complicated or time-consuming. Below are two simple exercises that you can easily integrate into your daily life to support emotional well-being.

Body Scan Meditation

1. Find a quiet, comfortable place to sit or lie down. Close your eyes and take a few deep breaths, allowing yourself to relax.

2. Begin by bringing your attention to your toes. Notice any sensations—whether it is discomfort, warmth, or stiffness—and allow yourself to simply observe what you feel without judgment.

3. Slowly move your awareness up through your body, focusing on each area in turn: your feet, legs, hips, stomach, chest, arms, and head. As you do this, consciously release any tension you may be holding.

4. If your mind wanders, gently bring it back to the part of your body you are focusing on. Complete the scan by taking a few deep breaths to ground yourself in the present moment.

5. Finish by stretching gently and slowly returning

your attention to your surroundings.

Breath-Focused Mindfulness

1. Sit in a comfortable position with your feet flat on the ground and your hands resting in your lap. Close your eyes and take a few deep breaths.

2. Begin to focus your attention on your breath. Notice the sensation of the air entering through your nose, filling your lungs, and then leaving your body.

3. As you continue breathing naturally, observe the rise and fall of your chest or abdomen. If your mind begins to wander (which is normal), gently redirect your focus back to your breath without frustration.

4. Stay with this awareness of your breath for 5–10 minutes, allowing yourself to be fully present in the experience.

5. When you are ready to end, take a few final deep breaths, then slowly open your eyes.

Guided Imagery Meditation Script

Another form of meditation that you might enjoy is guided imagery. Through this exercise, you can spend a few moments in a mental safe haven where you can find a sense of peace and calm, which is grounding and can help break you out of negative thoughts. If you'd like to try it, give this script a go:

Take a few deep breaths. Inhale slowly, allowing your chest to expand, and then exhale fully, releasing any tension as the air leaves your lungs. Let your breath settle into a steady, gentle rhythm, releasing a bit of tension from your body with each exhale.

Now, imagine a safe, calming place where you feel at ease and where everything around you brings comfort. It might be a garden filled with flowers, a warm beach with soft waves, or a quiet forest. Picture every detail—notice the colors, the sounds, the textures, and the scents. Feel the peace and warmth of this environment surrounding you. Let yourself be fully present here. This space is here to hold you and allow you to relax fully.

When you feel ready, imagine your pet in this peaceful place with you. Picture them however they were in their happiest moments, visualizing their bright eyes, their warm fur, and their joyful energy. Notice any small details that come to mind, like their favorite expression, the softness of their fur, or the sound of their purr or bark. Feel their presence here with you, as if they are right beside you. Maybe you can feel their gentle weight against you, hear their comforting noises, or simply sense the familiar warmth of their spirit.

Now, spend a few quiet moments connecting with your pet. Imagine looking into their eyes, feeling the bond you shared, and sensing the love they had for you. If it feels right, you can imagine reaching out to hold them or gently petting them. Pay attention to any feelings that come up. Perhaps it's gratitude, love, maybe a bit of sadness. Let whatever surfaces be here without judgment. It's okay to feel a mix of emotions; this is your moment to honor your connection with your pet.

Take this time to express anything you'd like to say to them. You can share words of love, let them know how much you miss them, or tell them how they impacted your life. Speak to them from your heart and allow any emotions to flow naturally. If words don't come, that's okay, too. Simply let yourself be in their presence and feel the connection that lives on between you.

Now, envision that your pet offers you a final, comforting message—a gesture, a look, or a feeling of love and peace. Take in this message, and as you do, feel their love filling your heart and bringing a sense of calm. When you feel ready, begin to gently say goodbye for now, with the knowledge that this safe space will always be here for you whenever you want to return. Feel gratitude for the time you shared and for the lasting love that remains in your heart.

When you're ready, slowly bring your awareness back to your breath, taking a few deeper inhales and exhales. Begin to notice your surroundings, the feeling of where you are seated, and the sounds around you. When you feel ready, open your eyes gently.

If you are interested in diving deeper into these practices, apps like Calm and Headspace offer great resources, and there are many free online videos that can walk you through guided meditations.

Coping Tools for Anxiety or Rumination

When grief is still fresh and a loss is recent, anxiety and rumination can be a significant consequence. You might feel overwhelming worry about the future and what it holds or find yourself unable to stop thinking about the same situations or circumstances over and over. Because this can be particularly distressing, it's good to have a few different coping tools at the ready to quell these anxious feelings.

Box Breathing

Box breathing, sometimes called square breathing, is great for regulating your breathing and calming your mind through a simple pattern. It activates the parasympathetic nervous system, which means that it can slow down your heart rate and help you feel calmer. To use this technique, inhale while you count to four, hold your breath for another four counts, exhale for four more, and hold for four again. As you're completing each cycle, visualize drawing a square as you breathe, with each side representing one step of the exercise. Repeat this sequence until you feel more at ease.

The 4-7-8 Breathing Technique

Another breathing technique is the 4-7-8 technique, which works similarly to box breathing. The key difference is how long each part of the breath takes. The longer exhalation period helps expel more carbon dioxide, which slows your breathing and reduces anxiety by allowing more oxygen to enter your bloodstream, thus calming both your mind and body. To engage with this technique, breathe in through your nose for four counts, hold for seven, and exhale completely through your mouth for eight. Repeat this process for three or four cycles or until you feel calmer.

The 5-5-5 Grounding Technique

Grounding, as we talked about earlier, can be helpful to pull you out of an anxiety spiral or a cycle of rumination. When you're trapped inside your head, grounding pulls you back down to Earth. This method helps you use physical sensations to feel more connected to your surroundings. To use it, you'll name five things you can touch (and actually touch them, noticing the sensations as you do), take a close look at five things you can see, and then take five deep, controlled breaths with a mindful approach.

Breath Counting

You can also use breath counting to reduce anxiety or draw your thoughts back to the present moment. This practice means that you can keep your mind focused on a soothing cycle that breaks patterns of rumination or anxiety by creating inner calm. To use this method, count each time you breathe in and out. Your first inhale would be one, your first exhale would be two, your second inhale would be three, and so on. Count up to 10 as you focus on your breathing and return your mind to the counting process if it wanders. Once you reach 10, you can start over if needed.

Time in Nature

Finally, spending time in nature can be immensely helpful when it comes to reducing anxiety and rumination surrounding the loss of a pet. Connecting with nature can help you find stability, peace, and comfort as you connect with the world around you. I particularly love sitting outside while doing breathing exercises. Sitting quietly as you take slow, deep, and intentional breaths can be healing. As you do so, notice the sounds, colors, and movements around you—leaves rustling, birds chirping, the sun's warmth, or whatever else is in your environment.

Crafting Mementos and Memorials

Mementos and memorials can help with healing, too, as the tangible reminders you create can offer immense comfort during the grieving process. Because these acts are meaningful ways to honor a beloved pet, they help you keep their memory alive and maintain a sense of ongoing connection.

Different Types of Mementos and Memorials

There are many different types of memorials and mementos you can create in honor of your pet's life:

- **Photo albums or scrapbooks:** You can create photo albums or scrapbooks to honor your pet's memory. To do this, collect your favorite photos of your pet and compile them into an album or use them to create a scrapbook. Include captions, notes, or stories that highlight the special memories you shared. This project is a way to celebrate your pet and a beautiful keepsake to revisit whenever you want to remember them.

- **Custom jewelry:** Custom-made jewelry and other items, such as necklaces, bracelets, or keychains, can be a subtle but deeply personal way to carry your pet's memory with you. You can potentially engrave their name, add a paw print, or even incorporate a small amount of their ashes into a wearable item if you'd like.

- **Shadow box:** Create a shadow box filled with meaningful items, such as one of your pet's toys, a paw print, and photos. This keepsake can be displayed in your home as a tribute to their presence in your life.

- **Memorial garden:** A garden can be a living, growing reminder of your pet. Plant flowers, shrubs, or a tree in their honor, choosing species that hold symbolic meaning for you. For example, rosemary symbolizes remembrance, while forget-me-nots represent love and memories that will never fade.

If you have other ideas for what you might want to create, absolutely feel free to do so! The bond you shared with your pet is special and unique, and that's something you can honor in any way that feels right for you.

Healing does not come overnight. It is an ongoing process that requires consistent effort, which you can now work toward using a combination of the strategies in this chapter. It is okay if you feel like certain methods are not working as well as others but be sure to give each one a genuine try and some time to work its effects. With that said, remember that your healing journey is your own; you are more than welcome to find what suits you best as you recover from your loss.

Chapter Four

Stories of Shared Experiences

*Everyone is taught that angels have wings. The
lucky ones of us find that they have four paws.*
–Jury Nel

B efore we move on to more tips for healing and accepting the loss of your pet, I want to spend a few
moments sharing some personal accounts from others
who have gone through similar experiences. These stories
are not here to sadden you but rather to show you that
grief is a normal, human thing to experience and that you
are not alone. For me, it was deeply healing to realize this
through what others have shared. If you feel like reading
them might be too much for you right now, though, feel
free to skip this chapter.

The Dog Who Taught Me Unconditional Love

This first story is about Anne's experience, a woman who suffered the loss of her beloved dog, Bailey. Here is what Anne wanted to share:

When I first met Bailey, I was at one of the lowest points in my life. It had been months since my divorce, and the empty house felt unbearable. Every evening, I'd come home to silence, and it was so incredibly isolating. That's when I decided to visit the local animal shelter. I wasn't sure if I was ready for a pet and the responsibilities that came with one, but the loneliness was becoming suffocating.

Bailey wasn't what I'd been expecting. She was older, her golden fur graying at the edges, and she had the wary look of a dog who'd been through a lot in her life. Her previous owners had surrendered her after moving out of state, which left her confused and heartbroken. But when she saw me, something shifted. She didn't bark or whimper. She just sat there like she was saying, "I'm lonely, too." Then and there, I decided to take her home. Little did I know that this scruffy rescue dog would change my life in ways I couldn't have imagined.

Every day, she'd wait for me by the door, her tail wagging excitedly. No matter how late I came home, no matter how tired or frustrated I felt, Bailey was always there for me. There was one evening in particular that I'll never forget. I had caught a terrible case of the flu, the kind that keeps you bedridden for days. Bailey knew something was wrong. Instead of running around or asking for her usual evening walk, she quietly curled up beside me on the couch. She stayed there for hours, knowing by instinct that her presence was exactly what I needed.

Unfortunately, the years passed more quickly than I'd anticipated. Bailey's energy began to fade, and her steps became slower. Still, she waited for me every evening by the door, even when her arthritis made it difficult for her to move. Her loyalty was unbreakable, and I valued that until the very end.

The day I lost Bailey, the house returned to silence. Her empty bed, the missing sound of her paws on the floor—it felt as though my heart had a hole in it. There was no wagging tail to greet me at the door, no comforting weight beside me on the couch on hard days. The house felt even emptier than it had before she entered my life.

In the weeks that followed, I became consumed by my grief. I couldn't walk past her favorite spot by the window without breaking down. But slowly, I realized that I needed to find a way to honor the love she had given me. So, I began to create a photo collage of all our happiest moments together, like our carefree walks in the park, her playful antics in the backyard, and the way her eyes sparkled with joy every time we were together. That project became my way of remembering the life we'd shared. I also planted a tree in the backyard, a small oak, right where she always used to sit and watch the birds. Every time I look at it, I imagine her there, still watching over me.

Bailey taught me many things, including patience, resilience, and the power of being present, but above all, she showed me what unconditional love truly means. She entered my life at a time when I thought I had nothing left to give, and in return, she filled my days with warmth and joy. Losing her was one of the hardest things I've ever experienced, but the love we shared will always be with me.

The story of Anne's beloved dog, Bailey, is one that sticks with me. It is so important to know that we are not alone. Just like Anne, many people find companionship in pets and feel the loss of those companions when they pass away. However, just like Anne, you can find ways to memorialize your pet and keep their love and lessons with you as you heal.

A Cat's Comfort in Times of Trouble

For this next story, I want to share with you what Darren experienced when he adopted and shared his life with a lovely cat named Luna:

I had always considered myself a dog person, but everything changed when Luna entered my life. She was a small, gray tabby with piercing green eyes and a calm attitude. I adopted her shortly after my father passed away, a time when I was struggling with grief and feeling lost. Luna seemed to understand from the very beginning that I needed the kind of comfort no one else could provide.

Whenever I felt overwhelmed by sadness, Luna would sense it immediately. Without fail, she'd appear out of nowhere and curl up in my lap. It was as if her purring had a magical effect, calming my anxiety and providing a sense of peace I hadn't known in months. I found myself crying less when she was near. Her quiet presence reminded me that I wasn't alone, even in the darkest moments.

Luna had unique quirks that made her impossible not to love. She had this endearing habit of pouncing up to join me the moment I sat down to read a book. She'd stretch herself luxuriously, her paws occasionally batting at the pages when I tried to turn them, which always made me chuckle. She made these adorable chirping noises at me when I woke up or went to feed her. But it wasn't just her calm presence that comforted me—Luna also had her playful side. She loved chasing beams of sunlight across the floor and would leap in the air, all silly and not quite co-ordinated. That brought much-needed laughter into my life during a time when joy seemed hard to come by.

Losing Luna was heartbreaking in ways I hadn't anticipated. The space we'd shared felt hauntingly quiet without her soft padding footsteps, and I often found myself listening for the comforting sound of her purring at night, but it never came. The routines we had—her hopping onto the bed as soon as I lay down, the way she'd stare at me with those green eyes as if she understood every word I said—were gone. I missed her nestling into the crook of my arm, her little body fitting so perfectly in the space that now felt empty. The absence was more than physical; it felt like I'd lost my confidant, the one who had quietly listened to my grief and given me solace without judgment or expectation.

Coping with her loss was difficult, and it took time for me to accept that the rituals we shared were now memories. But I knew I had to find ways to keep her spirit close. I framed a photo of Luna that I'd taken on a sunny afternoon when she was lounging by the living room window, her eyes half-closed in contentment. The photo now sits on my bedside table. I also found peace in writing about her and to her in letters. I knew I'd never send them, but they helped me express the gratitude and love I felt for her.

One evening, I wrote a poem in her memory. It wasn't much, but it felt like a way to honor her, to keep her memory alive in the words I chose. In some ways, Luna is still with me. Her spirit lingers in the quiet moments when I sit in her favorite spot, watching the sunlight dance across the floor, just like she used to. And though her absence is deeply felt, I take comfort in knowing that she gave me a gift that lasts beyond her time with me:

the gift of quiet, unconditional companionship when I needed it the most.

Darren and Luna's story goes to show that cats can be the greatest of companions, and even when you're facing the loss of a beloved friend, even if that friend is an animal, there are ways to heal. I particularly love Darren's story because it's inspiring: In honor of his peaceful but playful cat, he found equally meaningful ways to honor her, and that's very special.

Write Your Story

If you feel ready, I want to encourage you to write your own story about your pet and the ways you're working to heal from their loss. Like Anne's and Darren's, yours doesn't have to be a story that ends with being completely healed. It just needs to be a story that helps you explore your connection with your pet and where you are right now in the healing process. Think about what you'd like someone else to know about them and your relationship with them and what you'd like to share with anyone going through the same type of loss.

Hearing the stories of others may be saddening, but it's also an important way to know that you aren't alone. While every loss is different, knowing that others feel similar to how you do and that they've found a sense of peace and stability can help you come to terms with a loss and find healthy ways to heal. If you'd like to share your story or read the stories of more people, there are so many online platforms like Reddit and Facebook that can help. Remember, your story doesn't need to be perfect—it just needs to represent your experiences in a way you find meaningful.

Chapter Five

Professional Insights and Group Support

Until one has loved an animal, a part of one's soul remains unawakened. –Anatole France

It's deeply empowering to work toward healing as an individual, but there are also times when the support of others can make a world of difference. The insights professionals offer and that you encounter in group settings can help you access considerations, skills, and guidance that you might not come across or think of on your own. This is why this chapter is here. Its purpose is to help you gain an understanding of how external support can aid in your journey toward healing from the loss of your beloved pet.

Evidence-Based Coping Mechanisms

Evidence-based coping mechanisms are approaches that professionals have researched vigorously and that have proven efficacy when it comes to emotional healing. This means that these methods can be especially helpful during troubling times in our lives, including when we are grieving the death of a pet. Such approaches can be adapted to meet different needs and have shown their worth in helping with emotional regulation, stress reduction, and long-term resilience. There are many different types of evidence-based coping mechanisms, but two of the most well-known and valued include cognitive behavioral strategies and mindfulness.

Cognitive behavioral strategies are taken from what is taught in cognitive behavioral therapy (CBT). They come from the idea that our emotions are often rooted in flawed thinking. This does not mean that your grief is flawed but rather that you may be unfairly placing blame on yourself or otherwise thinking about circumstances in a way that prevents you from healing. CBT strategies allow you to view your experiences through a more logical lens, which is known to help during periods of mourning. This is because such strategies can challenge unproductive thoughts and help you shift toward acceptance.

Similarly, mindfulness techniques help you find a sense of grounding in the present moment, which counteracts being trapped inside your mind with thoughts that may be doing you more harm than good. These strategies can regulate your body by calming the nervous system, for example, which has a soothing effect on your mind. It also allows you to create a healthy distance between yourself and your grief so that you can process your experiences more objectively.

Progressive Muscle Relaxation

One evidence-based mindfulness method you can use is progressive muscle relaxation. This strategy involves tensing and relaxing different muscle groups in the body. When you do this, you can reduce overall tension because the exercise helps you feel more at ease by comparison. It is similar to how your bathroom light is always the same brightness but feels more glaring after you've spent eight hours sleeping in the dark. To perform progressive muscle relaxation, here's what you'll do:

1. Find a quiet space and sit or lie down comfort-

ably.

2. Starting from your feet, tense your muscles as hard as you can for 5–10 seconds, then release for 20–30 seconds, focusing on the sensation of relaxation.

3. Gradually move up your body (legs, abdomen, chest, arms, then face) following the same pattern.

4. Focus on your breath and how your body feels after each release.

Be sure to only tense your muscles as much as you comfortably can. Forcing yourself to clench too hard can be painful or cause cramping in different parts of your body.

Cognitive Restructuring

Another wonderful evidence-based method, specifically when it comes to CBT techniques, is cognitive restructuring. This strategy involves identifying thoughts that are inaccurate or unhelpful and shifting them to be more positive or balanced. Here's how you can do it:

1. Start by thinking about some thoughts you have

about the loss of your pet that are not helpful for your healing or actively produce negative
feelings. For example, something we discussed in
Chapter 2 is that a lot of people think that their
pet's death was their fault. This is not true, and
it's a belief that can be reframed.

2. Try to determine if there is any evidence supporting your thought. This might sound strange
but trust me here! Running with the thought
from Step 1, you might be tempted to think,
I could've noticed my pet was sick sooner. Is that
true, and would you ever ignore your pet being
sick?

3. Now, think of all the evidence that disproves
this harmful thought. For example, you did not
make your pet sick, you did not ignore their
symptoms, and you tried your best to care for
them—all of which means their death was not
your fault.

4. Finally, try to create a more accurate statement
that replaces the thought you've been working
with this whole time. Instead of thinking, *It is*

my fault my pet died, it would be more balanced to think, *I did everything I could for my pet, and their death was out of my control.*

Over time, cognitive restructuring has major benefits. It might not help to work with it just one time; rather, it's an activity you should try to engage with each time you notice a negative or unhelpful thought affecting you. For a more sustained and beneficial experience, you can even make this a journaling activity, where, at the end of the day, you restructure some of the negative thoughts you had.

Expressive Writing

Another strategy that you can use to understand and process your emotions through evidence-based techniques is expressive writing, as putting your feelings down on paper can improve your well-being immensely. This can help you put your thoughts and feelings into words in a way that is more conducive to healing than just thinking about those experiences. For this exercise, you'll need to:

1. Set aside 15–20 minutes each day to write about your feelings surrounding the loss of your pet.

2. Write freely—don't worry about grammar or structure. Focus on your emotional experience.

3. Allow yourself to explore deep feelings, even if they are difficult or uncomfortable.

4. Continue this practice daily or do it a few times a week, using it as an outlet for your grief.

Art Therapy

Art therapy is also an evidence-based strategy, and it can help you express your grief visually rather than verbally. This is an incredible technique for difficult emotions that may be hard to process or put into words. Beyond that, the simple act of creating art can help you find comfort in a project, turn it into a way to memorialize your pet, or otherwise channel a sense of calm. To engage in art therapy, all you need to do is gather whichever supplies you prefer—such as paints if you like painting, pencils for drawing, or collage materials if that's more your style—and then create a piece that reflects your current emotional state. When you're done, reflect on what your art says about what you're experiencing internally.

The Role of Therapy in Healing

For a lot of people, therapy might not be their first-choice option. There is a lot of stigma surrounding seeking professional help and the people who choose to participate in counseling, but you shouldn't let that stop you from healing. So many people go to therapy, from other pet owners to people who just want expert insights. Even if cost is a concern, there are resources like insurance, government assistance, sliding scale options, and more that can make therapy accessible, be it online or in person.

But why should you consider therapy for healing from the loss of a pet in the first place? Well, there are a few reasons. Chatting with a professional means that you have a safe space to express your feelings without worrying about judgment or having your emotions dismissed, which can be a concern for many people when it comes to sharing grief-related feelings about a pet with friends or family. A therapist can help validate the bond that you had and ensure that you feel understood. Furthermore, professionals are equipped with tools to help you navigate emotions such as guilt, sadness, and anger. They guide you through the grief stages while offering personalized coping strategies, which can help you move forward without feeling overwhelmed.

When you seek out treatment related to grief, there are a few different types of therapy that may be offered. Some therapists specialize in certain methods, while others have a few different forms of counseling that they work with. Most commonly, grief counseling will be offered as a specific form of therapy, or you may be encouraged to work with CBT or even art or music therapies. It depends on what you think will be most beneficial and the specific struggles you're facing.

Finding the Right Therapist

Finding the right therapist is a big deal. You want to find someone who you feel safe with and can trust with your deepest feelings, as well as someone who is credible and capable of helping you heal and grow. For many people, this process can feel overwhelming, but there are a few things you can consider beforehand to make your selection more intuitive.

First, you're going to want to think about some key logistical considerations. Do you want an in-person therapist or a telehealth professional you can meet with from home? What kind of budget do you have, and do you have insurance? From there, you can begin searching for professionals who meet your basic criteria and then start scoping out who might be the perfect fit. Some questions you may want to ask a potential therapist include:

- Do you have experience working with clients who are grieving the loss of a pet?

- What therapeutic approaches do you use for pet grief?

- How will you help me process the unique aspects of my bond with my pet?

Next, you can begin making an informed decision about the professional you feel is right for your needs. Book a consultation, and if you walk away feeling that someone isn't the right fit, keep looking! It's important to find a professional who makes you feel comfortable and who you can trust, even if the first one or two you contact aren't right for you. Once you've found a therapist you feel good about, be sure to attend appointments regularly and, to receive the best support, be open and honest during your sessions.

Janie's Success Story

I want to share a success story with you to help you see how you can find healing through therapeutic methods. Janie was the owner of a bunny named Blossom, and their relationship was strong. A lot of people think bunnies aren't very friendly or capable of forming emotional bonds, but Janie could tell you that that's simply not true; bunnies are simply different, but the connection between them and their owners isn't devoid of meaning.

When Janie lost Blossom, she felt her grief intensely. Blossom, who had come from a less-than-kind owner, warmed up to Janie, and they both found unconditional love in one another. She and Blossom would play together after work, and Janie felt immense peace after stressful days when she held her bunny. Naturally, after Blossom passed, Janie was heartbroken. After taking a few weeks to reflect, she decided to seek professional help—after all, many others had success with therapy after pet loss.

She started with a CBT therapist, and through the work they did in her sessions, she was able to reframe the blame she placed on herself regarding Blossom's death. She came to realize that there was nothing she could've done differently and found solace in the fact that she had done her best to give Blossom the life she deserved. Janie also tried art therapy to help her cope with the feelings she still wanted to express after CBT had helped her develop a healthier mindset. She discovered how much she loved painting, which led to many memorial paintings of Blossom that now hang around Janie's home.

Healing wasn't a quick and easy process, but Janie feels that therapy made a world of difference for her. She hadn't realized that self-blame was getting her nowhere and that there was immense power in sharing her experiences with others. By getting professional help, she has made major strides toward feeling better while honoring Blossom's memory, a reality that therapy can also help you create.

Group Support: Finding Community in Shared Loss

Group support is also very helpful during challenging times, like when you're grieving a pet. It can make you feel very vulnerable to lean on others, especially strangers, but there are many benefits in doing so. For example, the sense of community and shared understanding that you gain in these environments is powerful. Feeling understood without having to explain everything is uplifting because you know that other people, most of whom have been through the same things, just get you. You can discuss losing a pet openly in groups for pet grief, and everyone understands the pain you carry.

Moreover, the members who belong to a grief-based support group can encourage you, share coping strategies, and offer a safe place to vent about what you are experiencing. This level of support can be challenging to find elsewhere, especially if your close friends or family have never experienced pet loss first-hand or been impacted by it to the same extent. Hearing how others have managed their grief can provide hope and remind you that healing is possible, even if the journey is slow. You can also form long-lasting friendships and offer support in these groups, making the environment even more fulfilling and positive for yourself and others.

Different Types of Group Support

Many different types of support groups for owners grieving their pets exist, but the two main ones you'll find are in-person and virtual groups. The first kind involves face–to–face meetups that often take place in community centers, pet shelters, and sometimes even places like churches. For many people, this option is ideal because the meetings provide a sense of connection and comfort only found by being physically present with others. The dedicated space—both physical and emotional—provided can be healing and conducive to stronger bonds.

However, some people aren't ready or able to join these groups, or they simply don't want to—and that's okay. This is why virtual groups are an incredible option. Remote support groups often connect people on forums, social media, or through platforms like Zoom. It is very convenient if you do not have a way to attend in-person meetings, such as because of time constraints, distance, or other restrictions. These groups can also help you maintain anonymity if you are interested in that aspect.

Finding and Joining Support Groups

It can seem tricky to find and join a group, but don't worry—I have guidance to offer! If you are looking for an in-person group, try asking around at local organizations like community centers, rescue groups, and vet clinics. They may be able to offer a good starting point. Enquiring at libraries and churches or even asking a therapist can also help connect you to resources or point you in the direction of a group. You can even Google "pet grief support group near me" and find some options.

If you're looking online, there are so many communities dedicated to losing pets. For example, platforms like Facebook and Reddit host groups specifically created for grieving pet owners. This means you should be able to find a space to share stories, post photos, and receive support from others. If you'd rather have live conversations, you can find chatrooms and online communities that host video or text-based live sessions to join in on.

It is also helpful to consider things like the size of a group, the level of participation required, and who the group is led by. Some people prefer more intimate groups of only a few people; meanwhile, others prefer groups that are larger. Likewise, some people like to contribute to the discussion often, and others prefer when their fellow participants speak most of the time. Furthermore, some groups are led by therapists or grief counselors, and if you are looking for professional guidance in a group setting, this is something to ask about beforehand. Whatever you are looking for, there is a group out there to fit your needs and desires.

When you join a group like this, remember that receiving and giving support are equally important. You do not have to pitch in right away, but if someone is lending an ear to you, it never hurts to welcome them to do the same. Be sure to participate actively in the groups you pick to keep the community alive. Also, don't be afraid to be honest—the benefit of these groups is that others understand you and that there are people there to lean on. Finally, remember that the other participants are there for the same reason you are, which means that sometimes, the spotlight will not be on you. That's okay. Listening in can any way help you reflect on your own situation more deeply.

Online Resources and Support Groups

Online resources are important to explore as well. When you're grieving, it can be confusing to know where to go for help or certain information, but the internet is full of helpful guidance, information, and resources that can be used to aid with the healing process. The benefit of these resources is that not only are they cheap or free, but they are also accessible anywhere—day or night, whether you're settled in place or on the go, they are there for you. You can also find convenient options for professional services and hotlines that make it easier to access support than in-person choices might.

When it comes to virtual resources, you have hundreds of options, which might make it even harder to pick ones that truly help. If you are unsure of where to get started, here are some helpful places you can try first:

- **The Association for Pet Loss and Bereavement:** This site offers resources, articles, and support connections directed toward people like you and me who have lost a pet. They host free online chats that are led by trained facilitators to help people cope with their grief.

- **Rainbow Bridge:** This site is well-known for its comforting "Rainbow Bridge" poem and offers forums, articles, and memorial pages where pet owners can post photos and tributes to their lost companions.

- **BetterHelp:** This online therapy platform offers access to licensed therapists who specialize in grief, including pet loss. With flexible scheduling and the option for video, phone, or messaging sessions, it is an accessible resource if you are interested in seeking professional help.

- **Talkspace:** This is another online counseling service that connects people with licensed therapists. Talkspace offers a more structured plan where you can communicate with your therapist via text, audio, or video messages on a daily basis.

- **Reddit:** Reddit offers many different forums for users experiencing grief, including those who are healing from pet loss. These spaces are great for seeking support, sharing experiences, and offering advice of your own.

- **Facebook groups:** Similar to Reddit, Facebook has many groups that you can visit to connect with others who have lost a pet.

Starting Your Own Support Group

In some rare cases, you might find that your area doesn't really have very many support groups designated specifically for pet loss and supporting those who have lost a pet—or you may not align with the groups you're finding. In this case, it can be a great opportunity to begin one of your own if you feel ready. Starting a group can be a rewarding way to create a community, connect with new people, and provide a shared space for healing that others may be searching for as well. If you have the energy to lead a group, there are a few things to keep in mind to make the experience pleasant and fulfilling for everyone involved.

Goals and Purpose

The first step is to define the purpose and goals of your group. This helps shape the atmosphere and draws people who are seeking what your group can provide. For example, a lot of support groups for pet grief will focus on offering a safe space to share experiences, providing tools and resources for grief management, or building a community for mutual support. Try to outline why you're creating the group and what you are working to achieve in a short statement that highlights the benefits and unique focus you are aiming for.

Choosing the Platform or Location

Next, you're going to want to pick a location or platform through which you'll host your group. If you're operating online, you can use Facebook groups, Zoom, a Discord server, or another option that can be used for chatting, sharing stories or resources, and meeting over calls. Regular video sessions can provide meaningful and personal interactions between members, while message-based chat options can help those with different comfort levels stay involved. It's important to remember that online groups should be as private as possible to protect members and prevent insensitive people from joining and disrupting the group environment.

In-person groups will be a bit different when it comes to meeting locations. For example, libraries, community centers, pet supply stores, or even public parks can provide a relaxed, accessible environment for members. An open space is important to allow each member to feel comfortable and secure in the group. Be sure to set up seating and to take accessibility and comfort into consideration when picking your location as well. There should be wheelchair- and stroller-accessible areas and enough space for everyone to feel comfortable. You should also think about how often meetings will be held, such as weekly or twice a month, to maintain connection and to ensure space is available.

Finding Members

From there, you can focus on building up your group's membership. This might also look a little different online versus in-person. For example, you can search for members for an online support group by visiting various sites and spaces. Social media platforms like Facebook and Instagram can be a good place to advertise your group, including its goals and meeting times, if there are any. Forums for pet loss can provide a similar advantage. You can even ask animal shelters, animal clinics, and similar in-person spaces if they'd like to refer people to your group.

If you'd rather host an in-person support group, there are many ways to find members. For example, one great idea is to create and post fliers about your group. A lot of public spaces like community centers and libraries have bulletin boards where residents can announce different events. Local pet supply stores may allow you to leave fliers or host events in their spaces as well. It can also be helpful to ask veterinarian offices and animal hospitals—where a lot of people experience devastating news about a pet—to refer people to your group so that they can find the support they need.

Structuring Meetings

With the main details out of the way, the next consideration is the structure you'll have for each meeting. A good
meeting will start with welcomes and check-ins. This
can include having each member introduce themselves
and share why they're there. It doesn't have to be a deep
dive; these details can range from, "My name is Avery,
and I lost a pet," to "I'm Jason, and my cat died of old
age recently," depending on comfort level. The welcome
segment of meetings can also include a short check-in
where everyone shares how they're currently feeling.

For the main portion, some degree of structure can help
guide conversations and encourage sharing. You might
want to have themes for discussions, such as what the
first days without a pet were like, and to ask each member to share a similar story and reinforce community
spirit. Open sharing times are also helpful, though, to
ensure that participants can talk about what's important to them on a given day. Short activities like mem-
ory-sharing, mindfulness exercises, or journaling can
deepen the group's experience and provide structure as
well.

Finally, it's important to have a strong ending. This leaves members with a positive outlook and the desire to come back for future sessions. Asking a reflective question is a wonderful way to end and leave members with something to think about for their next session. You can also close by adding a positive touch through sharing words of encouragement or affirmations.

Being a Good Leader

Of course, when you're running a group, you'll want to be a good leader. It's important both for yourself and for your members, but what does it mean to be a strong leader in the first place, especially in this context? There are a few key elements to keep in mind:

- **Be empathetic and listen:** As a leader, it's important to listen to those in your group without judgment and to show empathy and validate them as they speak. While you can share your own experiences, it's important to stop yourself from overshadowing other members and rather focus on listening. Also, try to avoid attempts to "fix" a person's grief; they need a listening ear and supportive group above all else. Also, ensure that all responses from yourself and other members are respectful and kind.

- **Encourage participation:** A group can't thrive if no one is participating! As a leader, it's good to gently encourage each member to share something while also being mindful that not everyone is ready to open up. Offering chances to contribute comfortably and kind encouragement without pressure will create an active group where members feel safe with you as their leader.

- **Set boundaries:** Good leaders also make it a point to establish guidelines for mutual respect, confidentiality, and communication that keep every member safe and comfortable. If you'd like, a great way to implement this can be by setting aside a portion of your first meeting for everyone to share rules or boundaries they'd like enforced within the group.

- **Check in:** You can further improve the security of the space you're holding by checking in with members after a group session. If you noticed that a member seemed more upset than usual or shared something particularly distressing, talking to them once you've wrapped up can be a great way to help them feel seen and secure within the group.

- **Have resources and tools:** Finally, a good leader will have resources on hand to direct members to for further support, as well as coping tools to offer for use both inside and outside of the group environment. You can share grounding techniques, for example, to help members of the group cope during sessions that might be stressful or when troubling thoughts come up in their daily lives.

Overall, it is important to know that there are many options like professional and group support that can help you navigate such a complicated loss as the passing of a beloved pet. Whether you choose one or both options is up to you, but adding support from either to your journey can help the healing process move along more smoothly.

Chapter Six

Long-Term Healing and Ongoing Support

Love knows not its own depth until the hour of separation. –Kahlil Gibran

After the immediacy of a pet's loss has passed, a lot of people feel like that's the end of the healing process. Once the experience is no longer "fresh," it is tempting to think everything is fine and good and that you don't need to do anything more on your end to heal. However, this is often not the case. I remember feeling like weeks of good days meant I was done grieving, only to be blindsided by sadness when I least expected it, even years later. Healing is an ongoing process and requires sustained effort to be maintained. It is long-term methods and techniques for ongoing support that help prevent or manage these feelings as time passes, and this chapter is here to guide you in that.

Celebrating Anniversaries and Special Dates

Celebrating anniversaries is an important part of working toward long-term healing. The special dates surrounding your lost pet can be a heavy emotional weight, as they remind you of their life and death. This can make it challenging to feel positive around these times, but with the right mindset, birthdays, anniversaries, adoption dates, and more can be turned into special occasions to honor their life and the memories you shared.

You can celebrate and commemorate these dates to make them uplifting and a time for remembrance rather than grief. Many methods for this exist, so you can select one that feels most meaningful for you. It can be positive, for example, to light a candle to reflect privately on your experiences, write a letter to your pet, or think about your fondest memories of them. You can also hold a small gathering and invite others who loved your pet to share stories and support one another.

You can also make more outgoing efforts on such dates to honor your pet while bringing positivity and fulfillment to your life. For example, one way to pay tribute to their legacy is to give back. Organizing a small charity event, online fundraiser, or donation drive to benefit a local animal shelter or rescue group can be a great way to do this. You could ask family and friends to donate in your pet's name, which helps other animals in need and keeps your pet's memory alive in a meaningful way.

Personal Stories of Commemorating Special Dates

Sometimes, the best way to find ideas for how you might want to remember these dates is by hearing the stories of others who have done the same. For this reason, I want to share two brief stories from pet owners like you and me who have lost a beloved friend.

First, we have John, who owned a very upbeat, energetic dog who loved walking on mountain trails and exploring nature. After his dog's death, John found it hard to visit those same trails without difficult feelings surfacing. Following some time grieving and reflecting on his experiences, he decided he should not let his pet's passing hold him back from participating in the activities they used to do together and that he could continue to enjoy them in honor of his dog and his memory. From then on, John has made it a point to spend his dog's birthday and the anniversary of his death hiking the same trails they used to explore. When he does, John thinks about the fond memories they shared and the joy of spending time in nature, carrying his love for his dog with him all the while.

Another pet owner, Marie, had a cat as her companion. Naturally, because many cats are indoor pets, Marie did not have outdoor rituals with her cat. However, that does not mean she was unable to find ways to commemorate special dates. She decided to make it a tradition to dedicate an hour of her time on her pet's death date to remembering the bond they shared. Marie takes that opportunity to journal about memories, reflect on mementos like her cat's toys, and more. Each year, she also reads back the entries from prior years, which has become another source of comfort in this quiet, peaceful ritual.

Whether you decide to have a big ritual like a fundraiser or a small one in the comfort of your own home, using important dates in your pet's life to reflect or cherish the bond you shared can be meaningful and continue the process of healing as things change and as time passes.

Continuing Bonds: Keeping Your Pet's Memory Alive

When people think of losing someone, be it a pet or a human loved one, they often think that the bond with that individual ends when they pass away. That's not always the case. After all, bonds can continue even after someone is no longer physically with us. Realizing this is a valuable part of healing for many people. Finding ways to continue the connection between you and a deceased pet means that you can keep healing and finding meaning in that relationship despite their physical absence.

This does not mean pretending your pet is still around; it means finding ways to recognize how they are still a part of your life. Maybe they taught you unconditional love or helped you recognize that warmth is soothing in times of anxiety. Using the lessons you learned from them is just one of many ways to feel their presence even after they are gone.

Another way that you can achieve this is by creating a dedicated area in your home for mementos and memories of your pet. This can be something small like a shelf, a corner of a room, or some other space where you keep different reminders of them. Photos, collars, and maybe even a paw print are great items to keep in this space. This way, that space becomes a calming place where you can pause, reflect, and remember your pet on a regular basis.

You can also continue the bond you have with your pet by keeping a journal dedicated to them. Inside, you can write about your favorite memories, how you feel, what you've been experiencing in daily life since they passed, and more. You can even draw pictures of them or their favorite places. A journaling habit that becomes part of your self-care routine means that you can find time to regularly connect with your pet and preserve their memories, which you can always revisit in times of sadness or after many years have passed.

Working with ways to continue keeping a pet's memory alive and connecting with them even after their death is beneficial for so many reasons, which is why I recommend it. Nurturing these bonds can help you feel less lonely—a feeling that often accompanies grief. These bonds can also help provide joy and comfort as you reflect on positive memories and experiences shared with your pet.

Long-Term Strategies for Emotional Well-ness

Taking steps to ensure your sustained emotional well-being is just as important as anything else when it comes to healing from the loss of a pet. When you take the time to find long-term strategies that work for you and apply them to your daily life, it makes normal bouts of grief easier to manage and prevents it from resurfacing when you least expect it. Regular wellness practices mean healing and acceptance are easier to attain, and beyond that, they lead to resilience, which means experiencing grief without letting it define your life.

Long-Term Wellness Strategies

There are plenty of long-term wellness strategies that you can work with, but to give you a place to start, I'm going to share three of my favorites. First, we have exercise. Because exercise releases endorphins—something we talked about a bit earlier—working out or engaging with simple forms of movement can be a wonderful way to combat feelings of sadness or isolation while promoting happiness and stress-free living. This means that it can be a big help to pick physical activities that you enjoy and that easily fit into your life. Ideally, try to dedicate 20–30 minutes a day to this activity, but starting with 5–10 minutes can still make an impact.

You can also sustain your long-term wellness by picking up or reconnecting with hobbies and interests. A hallmark characteristic of grief that also corresponds with depression is a loss of interest in things you once enjoyed. Getting yourself out of that stage and refinding the ability to take pleasure in life means rekindling your interest in the world around you. One way to achieve this is by engaging in your hobbies, and they can be anything you want, as long as they are healthy and enjoyable. Creative activities like painting, writing, or making music allow you to process complex emotions in a safe and constructive way and can be a good place to start. Alternatively, hobbies related to your pet—such as making a scrapbook, knitting a memorial blanket, or baking treats for other animals—can provide a meaningful connection.

My final favorite way to sustain long-term emotional wellness is practicing self-compassion. Grief, especially when it comes to losing a beloved pet, can bring up a lot of negative feelings, and sometimes we wrongfully redirect those emotions onto ourselves. Instead of allowing them to fester, approach them with a compassionate mindset. Your pet would not want you to be mean to yourself, and negativity only prevents healing. Remember that your feelings are valid and that everyone heals at their own pace. You can also combat blame by reminding yourself that you might be distorting reality and need to work with the cognitive reframing techniques I shared in Chapter 5.

The Role of Self-Care and Mindfulness

Self-care and mindfulness also play a role when it comes to long-term emotional wellness. Taking the time to develop a regular self-care routine that includes relaxation and stress management can be helpful for maintaining a positive outlook and managing any negative emotions that arise. Practices like journaling about daily gratitude, spending time in nature, engaging in sensory activities (like aromatherapy or warm baths), or creating a bedtime routine that includes calming music or reading are great ways to achieve this and provide yourself with a comforting safety net for when things do get hard.

It is also good to establish a regular mindfulness practice for yourself, as this can help you focus on the present and how you feel without judgment. Techniques like mindful breathing, body scans, or simply observing your surroundings can relieve stress and support emotional regulation. Also, meditation can complement mindfulness by encouraging a state of calm where thoughts of your pet can surface naturally and be acknowledged gently.

Other Techniques

Groups and support networks are often overlooked when it comes to emotional wellness, but they can be a great tool! This might look like regularly attending a support or grief group that you've found, ensuring that you stay in contact with friends and family who are there for you, or even seeking out new friendships and relationships with understanding people. It is important to remember that support is a two-way street, which means that if you'd like someone else to be there for you, it is important to offer the same level of support in return.

It can also be healing to explore volunteer work or charitable actions. Your pet had a wonderful life under your care, but there are so many animals in shelters or without the resources they need. Volunteering and giving back to those who will benefit immensely from even the smallest acts of care can be a way to honor your pet's life and improve the lives of those who may be struggling. Anything from running a donation drive to volunteering to play with animals so that they remain socialized can make a bigger difference than you know—both for them and you.

Finally, make it a point to interact with your natural surroundings. Nature mimics the cycles we experience in our daily lives, including birth, death, and the joys that come in between. Spending time in the outdoors can help you feel connected to the ebbs and flows of grief while also allowing you to enjoy the scenery, feel interconnected with the world around you, and get enough sunlight to promote happiness and reduce anxiety. Taking a short walk in the morning or participating in a weekly sporting game can be a fun way to stay connected to nature and improve your mental health.

The Journey of Grief: Embracing Growth and Healing

Grief is a complicated, ongoing process, and so is healing. It is not something you focus on for a few weeks and then forget about; both are continuous, and you have to dedicate yourself to processing and working through them. Understanding this also means coming to terms with the fact that grief is not a linear process. You might have some days where you feel totally fine only to be struck with a depressed mood the very next day. This is completely normal and something to respond to with kindness and self-compassion.

Furthermore, it is important to know that while grief might feel especially troubling at first, the overall process and journey can lead to enhanced resilience and growth beyond what you might think possible. When you spend time healing after a loss, it can catalyze personal development by paving the way for the emergence of new connections, empathy, and strengths you did not know about before. So, while grief can be a difficult experience, the process of navigating through it can also have positive aspects and bring opportunities for growth.

But why should you embrace that change and growth in the first place? There are a few reasons. When you truly take the time to reflect on grief, it unlocks new perspectives and strengths that can be a guiding force. Many people feel that grief provides them with a new appreciation of life. When you lose someone, whether a pet or a human, you realize that your time on Earth is finite, and that can inspire you to make every moment count—to live not only in honor of your pet but also with a newfound respect for the gift of life. Plus, grieving allows you to see the world in new ways that can help you be kinder and more empathetic to others, which deepens relationships and helps create new ones.

Also, experiencing grief first-hand means that you can understand yourself and other people more deeply. If you've spoken about your loss with someone who has never had to deal with grief, then you know personally how difficult it can be to receive understanding in those situations. With your experience, you can connect to others and offer support in genuine, compassionate ways. You also gain an understanding of your own reactions to loss as well as the coping mechanisms that work best for you and how different emotions show up in your life.

Strategies for Embracing Growth and Healing

While grief can look different for everyone, certain strategies can help facilitate healing, personal growth, and long-term resilience. I highly recommend setting achievable goals and pursuing your passions. Exploring new interests or having something you're working toward can reinvigorate your life and give it direction. This might mean returning to an old hobby that provides a sense of joy and accomplishment. It may also involve something entirely new, such as joining a pet rescue organization or starting an animal-focused charity in honor of your beloved pet.

Reflecting practices can also be wonderful. Writing in a journal, meditating, and engaging in other reflective practices that you find helpful can allow you to keep observing the changes you experience, how they affect you, and how you respond to those situations. This means that you can look back on your growth and determine where more work or new methods might be beneficial.

Finally, it is important to create a support network for yourself, one that extends even beyond the scope of grief.

Having a support network means that you always have people by your side who you can trust and rely on, and you can fortify those bonds by offering the same in return. This group of people can consist of friends, family, other loved ones, and even professionals like counselors. Having a well-rounded, dependable support system where you know who you can rely on for what is a great way to embrace healing and growth by receiving consistent encouragement, assistance, and feedback.

Supporting Others Who Are Grieving

After having lost a pet, you know best what the experience is like and how heartbreaking it can be. Others around you may lose a pet for the first time, or they might lose one again while you're healing and growing, and it can be helpful for you and those close to you if you provide support where you are able to. Because you've been there yourself, you can show empathy and compassion in ways that not everyone knows how to.

Supporting others is an uplifting way to ensure your friends and family have the backup they need after a loss. With that said, there are a few things to keep in mind while you go about doing this. Although you've experienced the same thing yourself, each person grieves in a unique way, and this can cause you to forget how to support others. So, how can you be there for those you care about when they lose a pet?

Acknowledge But Don't Minimize

When someone loses a pet, it is easy for them to feel like their grief has been overlooked or underestimated. Since you've experienced this pain, you understand how deep it can go. Acknowledge their feelings sincerely by letting them know that it's okay to grieve a pet just as deeply as they might a human loved one. Similarly, avoid statements that might feel minimizing, like telling them they can get a new pet—you and I both know how hurtful hearing that can be. Listen, but don't try to fix it for them. Let them vent if you are comfortable giving them the space to and ask if there's anything you can do to help rather than offering solutions yourself. This will encourage your loved one to feel more secure and in control.

Share Your Experience

Sometimes, sharing your personal experience with pet loss can help others understand that healing is possible. It's not always appropriate to do this, though, because it can sometimes feel like you are making the conversation about yourself instead of the person in need of support. You should share your personal experiences if they are relevant. For example, you can validate how the other person feels by sharing a short explanation of how you also felt, then turn the conversation back over to them.

Offer Practical Support

If your friend or loved one is looking for practical support and is okay with you offering it, then that is an incredible way to help them feel cared for and stable as they grieve. This can come in many different forms, so ask what your friend might need to feel supported and help them out. For example, they might need help with chores, errands, or meals. They could also want someone to go through their home and remove all of their pet's items and store them for later to avoid seeing those reminders.

Provide Opportunities for Remembrance

Another way you can support someone who has lost a pet is by providing them with chances to share their experiences and memories when they feel ready. You can use this time to talk about how you honored your pet or help guide them through remembering them, but you should only do so when they are ready. You can invite them to share their favorite memories with you or suggest ideas like creating a memory box—or any of your personal favorites—to provide them with an outlet for their grief through remembrance.

Respect Their Grieving Process and Timing

Grief doesn't follow a set timeline. Some people might feel better after a few weeks, while others carry a deep sense of loss for months or even years. As someone who has been through it, you likely understand how complex and unpredictable grief can be. Even if their grief follows a different timeline than yours, stay supportive and kind and let them know you are there for them without expecting them to "move on" before they are ready.

Continue to Be Present Even as Time Passes

Grief, as you know, doesn't just up and vanish. It can come back years later. Similarly, being supportive doesn't end when someone starts having more good days than bad ones. Remain present, even after the worst is over. This means that the other person has a firm support group to rely on and that you'll have dependable people in your life to reciprocate when you need them.

Encourage Professional Support if Needed

Professional support is nothing to shy away from. If you notice that your loved one's grief is affecting their life significantly for more than a few days or weeks, it might be helpful to suggest help from a counselor or therapist. Since people can be scared off by this, try framing it in terms of what helped you. For example, I once told a friend, "You know, when I felt like this for so long, I reached out to a counselor who really helped me find new ways to cope, and it changed things for the better for me. Would you like me to help you find something similar?" This made her way more open to the idea.

Being there for someone who has experienced the same hardship you have is a great way to ensure they feel less alone. Although it may be tricky, think about how the people around you were there for you—giving that same care to others is both rewarding and life-changing for everyone involved. Remember, however, not to overexert yourself. If you are not ready to hear about the loss of someone else's pet, you don't have to be completely available. Let the person know that your pain is still strong, too, but you are happy to support them in other ways that are helpful to you both.

Personal Stories of Growth and Healing

Sometimes, the best way to understand how to integrate something into your own life is to see how others have done so. In what ways have real-world people embraced growth and healing? Let's take a look.

Let's start with the story of Ava, who lost her pet in an accident. Grief was a strenuous and long process for her. When she was ready, Ava started to embrace growth and healing, and she did so through volunteering at an animal rescue center. Although she started doing this in honor of her pet, over time, it turned into one of her greatest passions. Through her work, Ava helped foster and care for animals that might otherwise have had no chance at life, and she eventually adopted a new pet of her own. This experience was defining for her because it let her connect to people like her while also creating a habit of compassion and nurturing in her life—which extended to herself as well.

Another pet owner, Jose, lost his pet during an already difficult time in his life. He was experiencing many major changes, so losing his pet added to the crushing weight he felt. It was hard at first, but he eventually found solace in creative writing. Jose started writing these beautiful stories about his pet and the adventures she was going on in the afterlife. He also wrote about his experiences as someone who had lost a pet. He shared what he'd written in a support group one day and was encouraged to keep sharing his stories. He eventually started a blog, and other pet owners found comfort in his posts, which allowed Jose to connect to his innermost feelings and simultaneously provide comfort to others.

Embracing healing as a long-term process means that you do not have to rush into it. It gives you the time and space you truly need to explore your emotions, grow, and take advantage of some of the bittersweet positives, like compassion, that grief can bring about. It is important to remember, therefore, that grief and healing are journeys and not destinations and that committing to ongoing growth and self-improvement is the best way to honor yourself and your lost pet.

Chapter Seven

Moving Forward: When and How to Welcome a New Pet

Like a bird singing in the rain, let grateful memories survive in times of sorrow. –Robert Louis Stevenson

Welcoming a new pet into your home is a big decision. A lot of people feel like doing so is unfair or unjust when it comes to the pet who passed away. And if you're wondering whether getting a new pet is like replacing your previous one, the answer is no, it is not. Welcoming a new pet into your life is a way to create a new relationship with an animal friend. It does not erase, negate, or disrespect the bond you shared with a pet you had in the past. Having a new pet can also be healing and rewarding in many ways, and some people think of themselves as lifelong pet owners; they love having animals around all the time.

Whatever your reason may be, it is more than fine to welcome a new pet into your life, but it is important to know when you are ready so that the bond you create is healthy. You should also understand how to welcome a pet into your life after having lost one. Therefore, in this chapter, we are going to discuss everything you need to know in order to identify if you are ready for this step, as well as how to comfortably introduce your new companion into your home and life.

Assessing Your Readiness for a New Pet

Before welcoming a new pet, it is important to assess your readiness. This is important because, while some people find comfort in getting a new pet shortly after another one has passed away, it can often be a distraction from true healing. If your emotions are still too raw to provide the necessary emotional support, it can create a strained relationship between you and your new pet. Beyond that, unresolved grief can lead to viewing another animal as a replacement, which stunts your healing and is not fair to your pet. It can also lead to disappointment when you realize that they are not a replica of the pet you lost.

Also, grief can be draining. It can take a lot of energy from us and make it hard to take care of ourselves, much less an animal. Getting a new pet before you are ready can mean that they are not taken care of properly or that you sacrifice caring for yourself to have enough energy for them. Neither situation is ideal nor conducive to proper healing and growth, which is why assessing your readiness for a new animal friend matters so much. Ensuring that your desire is rooted in stability rather than wanting to alleviate the pain of grief will create a more positive experience for you and your future pet.

Self-Assessment Checklist

To help guide you through the process of assessing your readiness for a new pet, here are some questions you can ask yourself. This checklist is here to help you reflect on both your emotional state and your ability to commit to the long-term care of another animal.

- How do I feel when I think about my lost pet? Do memories bring a sense of peace and gratitude, or do they still trigger intense sadness or pain?

- Am I still actively grieving? Am I able to speak about my pet without overwhelming feelings of sorrow, or do I still feel like I'm in the depths of grief?

- What is motivating me to get a new pet? Am I looking for companionship and connection, or am I trying to avoid dealing with my emotions?

- Do I have the time and resources to care for a new pet? Am I ready to take on the responsibility of pet care, including feeding them, training them, and taking them for vet visits?

- How will I feel if this new pet doesn't behave the way my last one did? Am I prepared to accept a new pet as an individual, or do I feel like I'm looking for an exact replacement?

- Do I have a strong support system? If things get difficult, do I have friends, family, or professionals to help me adjust to having a new pet?

- Am I ready to invest in building a new relation-

ship with a different animal? Can I envision myself committing to the time and patience needed
to bond with a new pet, even if it's a different
experience from one I've had before?

Based on your answers, it is up to you to decide if you
can commit to a new pet in every way. If you still feel
like grief is placing too much of a strain on your life, you
can use your answers to the above questions to determine
specific areas in which you may need to focus on healing
and growth. Once you feel like the loss you experienced is
not affecting you too strongly each day and like you can
commit to the responsibilities of a new pet, you can begin
the process. But how do you know for sure that you are
ready?

Potential Indicators of Readiness

Beyond the questions above, there are a few other things
you can consider to decide if you are ready to take this
step. While your love for your past pet will never fully
fade, one way that you might know you are ready for a
new one is that the thought of having another pet brings
you excitement. If you think of adopting a pet as something joyful rather than seeing it as dreadful or feeling

neutral about it, that's a positive sign! Looking forward to forming a new bond and getting to know a new pet is a sign that your heart and mind are open to loving a new animal.

Another sign you might notice is that when you talk about the pet you lost, you no longer feel an overwhelming sense of sadness or dread. Instead, you might be able to reminisce about them fondly and even smile or laugh about the memories you shared. This does not mean that you've forgotten or "moved on" from them but rather that you've accepted the loss and can hold space for both the love you shared with them and the potential love you will have for a new pet.

Similarly, it is a big indicator of positive growth if you cherish the memories you had with your previous pet but can still look forward to and envision positive experiences with a new one. This shows balance and emotional readiness, which also indicates that you can honor the animal companion you lost while leaving space for future joy.

Finally, if you are ready for a pet, you might also find yourself excited about the idea of being a caregiver and nurturing an animal's life. For some people, after losing a pet, the idea of caring for another life sounds like an awful prospect. If you feel like providing love, safety, and attention would be uplifting and fulfilling, it might indicate that you're emotionally prepared to take on the responsibilities of pet ownership and offer the affection that a new pet will need to thrive.

At the end of the day, the biggest consideration involved in getting a new pet is whether you are ready to do so—and if you are not, being restrained enough to wait until you've healed more fully shows a great amount of strength. It is good for both you and any future animal you may own to be sure that you are ready to care for them meaningfully and consistently. By using the guidance above, you can do so effectively.

Honoring Your Lost Pet While Welcoming a New One

When you're grieving the loss of a beloved pet, it's natural to feel a sense of guilt or even disloyalty at the thought of welcoming a new one into your home. However, honoring your lost pet's memory can help provide a bridge between mourning their absence and opening your heart to new companionship.

Techniques for Balancing Honoring a Previous Pet With Welcoming a New One

Honoring your previous pet while welcoming a new one in a balanced way requires you to have healthy ways to celebrate the memory of the pet who passed away. There are so many different ways to do this. For example, you can create rituals or traditions that honor the memory of your pet in a structured way. This can be as simple as lighting a candle on the anniversary of their passing or as involved as holding an annual remembrance day. As we discussed in Chapter 6, rituals give you a sense of having an ongoing connection to your lost pet and provide emotional comfort by creating space for reflection, which helps you maintain a sense of continuity between the past and present.

In addition, you can keep memorial items in a special place to remind you of your lost pet. Physical reminders, as I've mentioned before, can be an effective way to both honor their memory and create a healing environment. Whether it's keeping their collar, a favorite toy, or something like a framed photo in a dedicated space, placing these items somewhere visible makes tangible symbols of the bond you shared more prominent. Having a special spot where you can go to remember your pet can offer comfort and keep their presence alive in your daily life, even as you form a new connection with another pet.

Creating a photo album or digital slideshow can also be a meaningful way to honor your previous pet. You can use options like these to showcase your favorite memories with your pet and caption them accordingly to provide you with a consistent, stable reminder of your love and experiences with them. You can then visit this memento as often as you want to so that it can remind you of your bond with that particular pet.

Some people prefer more of a living way to honor an animal companion's passing, and that's where planting a garden or tree in your pet's honor can shine. You can select different types of plants to create a vibrant representation of the love you shared with them. Tending to those plants in their honor is also a wonderful way to allow their legacy to live on even after they have passed away. Plus, this creates a comforting, beautiful space for remembrance and reflection.

Creating Balance

Now, you may be wondering how you can strike some balance between honoring your pet who has passed and fostering a relationship with your new one, and that's a totally valid concern! One thing you can do is make time for remembrance. Adjusting to a new animal, even if you are in a good place, can bring up feelings of grief once again, so setting aside specific times to reflect or remember your lost pet can help you grieve in healthy ways. Not only that, but this prevents grief from overshadowing your budding relationship with a new pet and balances your emotions in an uplifting way.

It's also helpful to allow yourself to form new bonds without feeling guilty. It's common to feel like you're doing something wrong as you learn to love a new pet, but it is important to remember that you can love many beings in unique ways and that loving one animal does not detract from the love you have for another. Just as loving a new person doesn't diminish past relationships, welcoming a new pet doesn't erase what you felt for your previous companion. In moments of guilt, reminding yourself that you can cherish both animals simultaneously is healthy and creates balance.

The Emotional Journey of Adopting Again

Adopting a new pet after losing one can bring up a lot of different emotions, which can make it confusing. You might feel excitement and trepidation as well as happiness and sadness all at once, which is completely normal. The anticipation of forming a new bond and experiencing the unconditional love of an animal again can feel exhilarating. However, this happiness may also be tempered by other emotions like guilt or longing, and that's okay.

Managing These Emotions

Even though you might be in a good place and feel ready to bring a new pet into your life, it is important to know how to manage the conflicting emotions you might experience in the event that they arise. Having these techniques in your toolkit means that you are prepared and can keep yourself emotionally grounded no matter what challenges come your way.

One effective way to achieve emotional management when it comes to grief or other upsetting feelings surrounding the adoption of a new pet is to exercise self-compassion. This means acknowledging that guilt and grief are natural while also coming to terms with the fact that these feelings do not diminish your love for a previous pet. When they surface, it is important to take a step back and remember that while all emotions are valid, how you treat yourself because of what you feel makes a world of difference. A compassionate attitude toward yourself will make the transition smoother.

Another helpful management strategy is to chat with a friend, supportive person, or professional about the feelings that are coming up when you think about or make strides toward adopting a new pet. Sharing these emotions with others can be a great way to gain some perspective on situations, receive empathy and comforting guidance, and ensure that you are well-supported on your journey.

Take It Slow

When you adopt again, it is important to allow yourself and your new pet the chance to take things slow. Rushing into the bonding experience can make it easy for difficult emotions to resurface and challenging for a true connection to form, which is why it is so important to recognize that a bond may not form overnight or even for a few weeks. Spend some time helping your pet get to know you slowly and allowing them to get used to their new environment. This will encourage a natural, comfortable connection between you and your pet.

Also, make sure that you are not pressuring yourself to be completely positive. Part of taking it slow means giving yourself the space you need to grieve your old pet while relishing the joys of having a new one. You are allowed to balance the two and give yourself a chance to heal within the dynamic of a new relationship with a pet, and that process, like bonding, does not happen overnight.

Choosing the Right Time and the Right Pet

With the previous considerations in mind, you might be thinking about how you can time the adoption properly and pick a pet that's truly right for you. Let's go over the key aspects of knowing when you are ready for a new pet once more:

- If you feel like you are stable emotionally, financially, and otherwise, then it might be a good time to introduce another pet if you want one—you certainly do not have to make up your mind now if you are not sure. However, consider work commitments, social obligations, and family dynamics. Pets require time, energy, and financial resources for proper care, so adopting a new one when you're going through significant life changes, like moving or starting a new job, may add unnecessary stress.

- If you feel like you can provide love, support, and care to a pet, no matter what personality they have or how affectionate they end up being, that's another sign you may be ready. If you're still deeply grieving and find yourself frequently upset by reminders of your lost pet, it may be wise to wait until you can think of them with more peace. Emotional readiness doesn't mean that you no longer feel sadness but rather that you feel capable of forming a new bond without comparing your new pet to the one who has passed away.

You might realize that you are not ready to welcome another animal quite yet, and that's okay. It does not mean that you'll never be ready; it just means you need to take more time for yourself and your healing.

Selecting the Right Type of Pet

When you're thinking about the type of pet you may want, it might be tempting to think of getting the same kind you just lost. After all, they were such a good companion that another one like them would be perfect, right? Well, not necessarily! A mentality like that is rooted in clinging to the past, and a new pet is a chance to refresh your life and continue moving forward, even with your past pet still in your heart. There are a number of things to consider when deciding which sort of pet is right for you now.

For example, think about various breeds and care requirements, no matter whether you are looking for a dog, cat, bunny, bird, or anything else. Different breeds and species have distinct needs and temperaments, which is important to consider in relation to the level of care you can and are willing to provide. Before choosing a pet, research exercise, grooming, feeding, and medical considerations. Think about factors like lifespan, size, and health predispositions to ensure that you can commit to long-term care. For example, some breeds may require vigorous exercise on a daily basis whereas others are more suited to a calm indoor lifestyle.

Also, a pet's energy level and personality should align with your daily routine and activity level. For instance, if you lead an active lifestyle, a high-energy dog breed, such as a Border Collie, might be a good match. On the other hand, if you prefer quiet evenings at home, you might be better suited to a laid-back pet like a senior cat or another low-energy kind of animal. Be sure to think about whether you'd prefer a pet who's more independent or one who seeks constant companionship as well.

The Importance of Compatibility

Taking the time now to consider what would make a pet compatible with you is important, as thinking about how well their needs and disposition align with your lifestyle and personality will ensure that the two of you get along well—or as well as possible—from the start. Some people prefer pets who are calm, affectionate, and content to relax by their side. Others prefer more playful and active pets who enjoy outdoor activities and mental stimulation. Think about what type of interactions and activities you enjoy most with a pet, and then choose one whose behavior will complement your lifestyle.

You should also think about the space and environment you have. Be sure that your home environment is appropriate for the type of pet you choose so that everyone is happy. If you live in an apartment, a large, high-energy dog may not be a practical choice. On the other hand, a smaller dog or a cat might live comfortably in a smaller space. However, if you have access to a yard or live near parks, you might be well-suited to a pet who enjoys spending time outdoors.

Introducing a New Pet to Your Home and Heart

Bringing a new pet into your home, especially after the loss of a beloved companion, is a big transition for both you and the animal you've taken in. Progressing gradually is necessary to ensure that your new pet feels safe and welcomed and that you, as the owner, have time to adjust emotionally and practically. Specifically, a slow and steady introduction to your home and heart helps reduce the stress your pet might feel from entering a new environment. It also means they have time to adjust without too many stimuli overwhelming their senses. Plus, taking enough time helps you get to know each other, including your personalities and preferences, without causing distress or, in your case, guilt or the surfacing of grief-related emotions.

Planning is helpful when it comes to a smooth introduction. Try setting up a comfortable and safe area where your new pet can adjust naturally. A space away from activity, such as running kids or adults bustling in and out of rooms, can help reduce anxiety, especially if their essentials—food, water, bedding, and toys—are near that quiet spot. If you have other pets or family members, it is helpful to allow everyone to meet in a neutral, calm space. Careful supervision is especially important when children and other animals are involved.

Patience and Consistency

Patience and consistency are two of the most important aspects of welcoming a new pet to your home and heart. Pets thrive on routine, so setting up regular schedules for feeding, bathroom breaks, and exercise can help them feel more settled and secure. Consistent mealtimes and daily walks for dogs or regular play sessions for cats can create a sense of predictability and stability. Having a routine also helps you establish a sense of normalcy and balance in your own life as you adjust to the new dynamic and continue to heal.

Furthermore, positive reinforcement is helpful for making your new pet feel comfortable and confident in their new home. This means rewarding good behaviors with treats, praise, and affection so that they become well-adjusted to your home. Along the same line, avoid punishment, as it can lead to fear and anxiety. Focus on building a trusting and loving relationship by encouraging exploration, curiosity, and interaction on your pet's terms.

Creating New Memories While Cherishing the Old

It is natural to want to continue to honor the companion you lost, but it is just as important to work toward a healthy relationship with your new pet. This does not mean forgetting about or not loving your previous pet but rather recognizing their impact while continuing to form new, positive memories for yourself. This is important for your well-being and can look like establishing routines that provide you with a sense of normalcy—such as walks, mealtimes, and play sessions—or general shared activities that encourage trust and companionship between the two of you.

There are so many different ways to create new memories. For example, depending on the type of pet you adopt and their comfort levels, outings or indoor adventures are fun and engaging for you and for your pet. A regular walk in the park or supervised outdoor time can be a great way for both of you to get fresh air and have some fun while bonding. Likewise, indoor activities that enrich and engage your pet, like playing with toys or fun training sessions, can lead to great memories and experiences.

It can also be meaningful to celebrate special dates, such as their birthday, adoption date, or even some holidays with them. Small traditions like giving or making them special treats, gifting them new toys, having photoshoots, and incorporating other ways to celebrate these dates can establish a habit of creating positive moments and memories during different points of the year.

Simultaneously, it is a good idea to find routine ways to celebrate the experiences you had with a previous pet to keep their memory alive in you and encourage healing moments for reflection, even as years pass following their death. You can do so in whatever way feels best—maybe revisit some of the ideas we discussed in Chapter 3 for inspiration. I love having a place to store mementos and meaningful items. For example, the memory box I created for Whiskers, which I still have, has his collar, favorite toys, photos, and letters I'd written to him. I've revisited it many times, especially when I was growing up. It's given me a tangible way to remember the good times we shared. You can also share photos and stories with loved ones to help keep your pet's memory alive.

Preserving Memories With a New Pet Before They Pass

When they bring a new animal into their life after having lost one, a lot of pet owners worry about the eventual loss of their new pet. It's completely normal to be concerned about this, but you can't live your life stressing about the future! This thought, at least, can be comforted by preserving memories you create throughout the duration of your new pet's life. Not only does this give you ample opportunity to enjoy life and experiences with them, but it also means that when they pass, you'll have plenty to reflect fondly on.

There are so many different ways to create memories with a pet while they're in your life. You can work with whatever methods and choices are best for you, but you can use these ideas to create meaningful memories if you're unsure of how to begin:

- **Photo albums:** Creating a photo album, whether physical or digital, can help capture and preserve everyday moments that you share with your pet. All of the images and videos you collect can seem like snapshots of just another day in the life now, but you can look back on them later and remember all of them fondly. This is also a great way to record their personality. You can get started with this by taking photos and videos of your pet during their favorite activities or quiet moments and then compiling them to look back on later.

- **Keepsake paw prints:** For animals with paws, this can be a wonderful memory to hang onto. Because paw prints are unique, creating an imprint means having a physical reminder of your pet. You can find kits online and use them to make an impression of their paw print or use nontoxic clay or pet-safe ink to make a paw print keepsake. You can display this as a framed memento or keep it in a special place.

- **Journals or memory books:** Writing about the experiences you share with a new pet can be another wonderful way to preserve memories as time passes. You can create a journal where you write about your favorite experiences, funny moments, habits you have with your pet, or even just everyday occurrences. Although a moment seems small now, you never know what you might appreciate looking back on in the future. You can also use your journal to write letters to your pet—I have a friend who loves writing letters about what their pet learned or did that day.

- **Memory boxes:** For a more tangible option, a memory box is a great choice. It can be a small but sturdy box where you keep some of the items your pet has loved, which means you can look back on them and reflect on the memories they hold. For example, if a favorite toy is retired because it was replaced or too worn, keep it in the memory box so that you can look back on all of the positive times your pet enjoyed playing with it.

- **Social media or blog posts:** As they say, the internet is forever. It's one of the few things that we can count on to always be there and remain consistent, which is why creating a social media page or blog dedicated to your pet is a great idea. There, you can share photos, videos, journal entries, and other information about them—which not only gives others a space to send love to you and your pet but also creates a place you can revisit down the line.

- **Rituals:** Establishing rituals to share with your pet can create fun experiences that translate to fond, meaningful memories. Rituals that you engage with alongside your pet, like a daily walk, treat, or quiet bonding moment, can be grounding and provide comfort. This also creates a strong relationship between you two.

- **Milestone celebrations:** Make it a point to celebrate milestones and important days in your pet's life, and you can even find ways for them to be present for celebrations on your own special days! Marking these occasions means that you have anniversaries to remember fondly and honor as time passes.

Introducing a new pet into your home can be a tricky situation to navigate, but it is something many people aim to do after losing a beloved companion. Once you know you are ready to support a new animal friend, slow and steady introductions, dedicated bonding experiences, and a positive outlook can make a world of difference in creating a positive environment for you both.

Conclusion

You've made it to the end of the book, and you should be proud of yourself for doing so. Grief is no easy thing to manage, nor is healing, but reading this guide shows that you're committed to finding peace and honoring the life you shared with your pet. It's never easy to lose a beloved companion, but now you have some of the techniques and insights necessary to begin the process of recovering from pet grief and allowing yourself to remember your pet in meaningful ways. Let's take a look at everything you learned. Together, we discussed

- what grief is, including an in-depth look at pet grief and how it can lead to a roller coaster of emotions. We also explored the scientific aspects of what grief is and how it works.

- the five stages of grief, including what each stage entails and an overview of key strategies for each of them.

* immediate strategies for daily grieving and finding points for healing through journaling, exercise, mindfulness, and more.

* many stories of pet owners who have overcome grief and experienced the challenges of coping with loss along the way—providing hope and the knowledge that you are not alone.

* the value of therapy and support groups in healing from the loss of a pet.

* long-term tools and techniques to support the ongoing journey toward healing, even when the immediacy of loss has passed.

* everything you need to know about adopting a new pet and how to acclimate yourself and them to one another to form a loving, positive bond.

It's important to remember that grief is an individual journey, which means that you have to find the strategies that work best for you, even if those aren't the same ones that work for others. So long as you're working toward healthy habits, remembrance, and creating positivity in your life, there's no right or wrong when it comes to healing.

Grief is a complex experience, but my hope is that I have offered some guidance that you can carry with you and use to heal. If you've found this book to be valuable to you or your growth, I would appreciate it if you'd leave a review! Not only does this help me out, but it helps others find this guide and the valuable content it provides, which is a wonderful way to give back and support others experiencing pet loss.

Before we part ways, I want to share a final story of a pet owner like you and me who lost a beloved companion. A lot of people think pets like birds aren't friendly and affectionate and that their death is not as impactful as the death of a cat or dog. For my friend June, this wasn't the case at all. Her bird—a gorgeous, colorful friend—passed away from old age overnight, and June was heartbroken. Her days had been defined by her pet. They'd played together, she'd fed him on a routine schedule, and her bird had always wanted affectionate pets and to chirp lovingly at his human friend.

When June lost her bird, she had a challenging time because it felt like no one really understood, even those who had also lost a pet. Not only had she lost her best friend, but she felt isolated from those around her who couldn't understand her experience fully. Navigating her grief was a hard process from the beginning, and she didn't know what to do. Slowly, however, June was able to come to terms with her loss by setting up a shelf for her bird, where she set their favorite toys, pictures, and sentimental items. She also journaled about her experience and created a digital archive full of photos and videos she had taken over the span of her bird's life.

Eventually, June thought about doing something more. Her bird was gone, but there were others out there who didn't have owners or who were being mistreated in shelters, and that broke June's heart. She wanted every bird to feel the same love and joy that her precious companion had during his life. Because of this, June was inspired to volunteer at a local shelter that had a lot of birds but low adoption rates. She spent a lot of time there, helping workers understand the specialized needs of these creatures, talking to potential adopters about the birds there, and ensuring each one got their social and physical needs met on a regular basis.

June was able to help so many birds. One day, she host-
ed an adoption fair through a social media campaign.
That day, every bird in the shelter found a perfect, loving
home, except for two who had to be adopted together.
After going through this journey, June realized that she
was ready for a new feathered friend and that maybe
those birds were left behind for her. She took them home
that night and still cares for them today.

Now, June has two new loving companions and divides
her time between caring for them and volunteering at
the shelter she now thinks of as a second home. She also
regularly honors her bird who passed by lighting a candle
and reflecting on their time together, viewing videos and
photos, and more. Sometimes, the pain is still there, but
June is in a much better place emotionally and is eternally
grateful for the life of her previous pet and the opportunities she's had to care for other birds.

Pet grief isn't identical for any two people. Whether you
owned a cat, dog, bird, or another type of companion,
your grief is very real and very valid, and you deserve to
heal and grow from that experience. Keeping the tools
and insights I've shared with you in mind will help in
this process. Remember that grief and healing take time

and that committing to this journey will be your greatest chance to grow and find resilience.

From one person who has lost a pet to another, my heart goes out to you. I know that it's never an easy experience, but it's one that I'm confident you'll be able to work through. Use what you've learned to honor and remember your pet and take care of yourself—you've got this!

Share Your Thoughts

Dear Readers,

I hope you've found comfort and guidance in this book. Your journey through grief is unique, and I hope this book has provided effective tools and insights to help you navigate it.

By sharing your thoughts and experiences, you can help others who are also grieving to know that they are not alone. Your review can offer hope and encouragement to those who may be feeling lost and overwhelmed.

To submit a review, kindly navigate to your Order History, locate the book in your purchased items, and select 'Write a Product Review.'

With gratitude,

Joyce T.

References

American Psychiatric Association. (2024, March 27). *How pets can protect cognitive health in older adults.* https://www.psychiatry.org/news-room/apa-blogs/pets-can-protect-cognitive-health-in-older-adults

Andriote, J.-M. (2021, July 7). *8 ways to sleep better when you're grieving.* Sleep Enlightened by Saatva. https://www.saatva.com/blog/grief-and-sleep/

AVMA. (n.d.). *Coping with the loss of a pet.* https://www.avma.org/resources-tools/pet-owners/petcare/coping-loss-pet

Borgi, M., & Cirulli, F. (2022). Companionship and wellbeing: Benefits and challenges of human-pet relationships. *The Palgrave Macmillan Animal Ethics Series*, 289–315. https://doi.org/10.1007/978-3-030-85277-1_14

Boyraz, G., & Bricker, M. E. (2011). Pet loss and grief: An integrative perspective. *The Psychology of the Human–Animal Bond*, 383–401. https://doi.org/10.10 07/978-1-4419-9761-6_22

Cherry, K. (2023, February 22). *What is attachment theory?* Verywell Mind. https://www.verywellmind.c om/what-is-attachment-theory-2795337

Clark, A. (2017, February 14). *The cultural stigma of pet loss and grieving their death*. Psychology Today. https://www.psychologytoday.com/gb/blog/animal -attachment/201702/the-cultural-stigma-pet-loss-an d-grieving-their-death

Coles, W. (2022, November 27). *A new perspective on grieving loss of a pet*. Neuroscience News. https://ne urosciencenews.com/grief-pet-loss-21950/

Dutes, K. (2023, July 25). *Life Kit: Losing a pet is hard. Here's how to cope*. NPR. https://www.npr.org/2023 /07/24/1189865100/processing-pet-grief-with-love

The Humane Society of the United States. (n.d.). *How to cope with the death of your pet*. https://www.huma nesociety.org/resources/how-cope-death-your-pet

Hvilivitzky, T. (2017, June 13). *The link between emotional support dogs and cortisol.* BpHope. https://www.bphope.com/pets/the-link-b etween-emotional-support-dogs-and-cortisol/

Jenny. (2023, October 17). *The cultural differences in attitudes towards cats around the world.* Oh My Sweet Cat. https://ohmysweetcat.com/the-cultural-differe nces-in-attitudes-towards-cats-around-the-world/

Marshall-Pescini, S., Schaebs, F. S., Gaugg, A., Mein- ert, A., Deschner, T., & Range, F. (2019, 12 October). The role of oxytocin in the dog–owner relationship. *Animals*, *9*(10), 792. https://doi.org/10.3390/ani91 00792

McGowan, R. T. S. (2024, September 20). *How can cats reduce stress and improve moods?* Puri- na. https://www.purina.com/articles/cat/getting-a-c at/how-can-cats-improve-moods-and-reduce-stress

Mental Health America. (n.d.). *I'm feeling too much at once: Dealing with emotional over- load.* https://mhanational.org/im-feeling-too-much -once-dealing-emotional-overload

Mindful Staff. (2024, March 18). *Mindfulness for grief and loss*. Mindful. https://www.mindful.org/mindfuln ess-for-grief-and-loss/

Nationwide. (2023.). *The paw-sitive mental health impact of pets*. Nationwide Companion Magazine. https://companionpetmagazine.com/issues/sprin g-2023/the-pawsitive-mental-health-impact-of-pets

Pets may help reduce anxiety & depression in young adults: Effects of dog & cat ownership (2024 Study). (2024, March 5). MentalHealthDaily. https://mentalhealthdaily.com/2024/03/05/pets-anxiet y-depression-young-adults-effects-dog-cat-ownership-2 024-study/

Smith, M., Robinson, L., & Segal, J. (2019). *Coping with grief and loss*. HelpGuide.org. https://www.helpguide. org/articles/grief/coping-with-grief-and-loss.htm

Telloian, C. (2019, October 22). *11 tips for a morning routine that supports mental health*. GoodTherapy. https://www.goodtherapy.org/blog/11-tips-for-a -morning-routine-that-supports-mental-health-

Tyrrell, P., Harberger, S., Schoo, C., & Siddiqui, W. (2023, February 26). *Kubler-Ross stages of dying and sub-*

sequent models of grief. National Library of Medicine; StatPearls Publishing. https://www.ncbi.nlm.nih.gov/books/NBK507885/

Williams, L. (2022, February 2). *What does it mean to integrate grief?* What's Your Grief? https://whatsyourgrief.com/what-does-it-mean-to-integrate-grief/

Wolfelt, A. (2023, December 21). *Helping yourself heal when a pet dies.* Center for Loss & Life Transition. https://www.centerforloss.com/2023/12/helping-heal-pet-dies/

Image References

ElvisClth. (2016, May 12). *Weimaraner, puppy, dog* [Image]. Pixabay. https://pixabay.com/photos/weimaraner-puppy-dog-snout-1381186/

guvo59. (2023, July 21). *European shorthair, cat, kitten* [Image]. Pixabay. https://pixabay.com/photos/european-shorthair-cat-kitten-pet-8136129/

Lepale. (2016, November 28). *Dog, labrador, pet* [Image]. Pixabay. https://pixabay.com/photos/dog-labrador-pet-canine-companion-1861839/

LePhuong0401. (2023, January 5). *Dog, pet, husky* [Image]. Pixabay. https://pixabay.com/photos/dog-pet-husky-puppy-outside-7691238/

wisshajj. (2023, January 5). *Rabbit, nature, bunny* [Image]. Pixabay. https://pixabay.com/photos/rabbit-bunny-hare-pet-ears-easter-7692466/

Made in the USA
Columbia, SC
21 April 2025